The Power of Three

The Power of Three

Endorsements

'A *fount of wisdom and a guide for life. Norman Drummond's philosophy of threes has inspired his own rich and varied life as pastor, headmaster, social entrepreneur and mentor to many. It will do the same for all those fortunate enough to read this book.'*
Charles Handy, international author and philosopher

'For people of faith and of none, The Power of 3 is an inspiring blueprint for enriching our lives. Norman Drummond has again shown us a clear path through a turbulent world.'
Sir Tom Farmer, global entrepreneur and philanthropist

'Norman Drummond is one of the leading social entrepreneurs in Britain. Over the years I have found both his wisdom and his practical insights to be a source of inspiration and encouragement. Norman does what he says and lives what he believes, very rare qualities these days. If you want to know what social entrepreneurship is about this book and this man will tell you.'
Lord Mawson OBE, author of *The Social Entrepreneur*

'In these times of change and disappointment when the drive of competition, commercialism and wealth are exposed as a false route to happiness, The Power of 3 is an illuminating and inspiring voice which, like a good friend, points to a new path of sincerity and unselfish purpose which rewards with joy and hope in life's journey.'
Mary Contini, celebrated travel and food writer

The Power of Three

Norman Drummond

HODDER &
STOUGHTON

First published in Great Britain in 2010 by Hodder & Stoughton
An Hachette UK company

2

A CIP catalogue record for this title is available from the British Library

ISBN 978 0 340 97991 4

Typeset in Sabon by Hewer Text UK Ltd, Edinburgh
Printed and bound in the UK by Clays Ltd, St Ives plc

Hodder & Stoughton policy is to use papers that are natural, renewable
and recyclable products and made from wood grown in sustainable
forests. The logging and manufacturing processes are expected to conform
to the environmental regulations of the country of origin.

Hodder & Stoughton Ltd
338 Euston Road
London NW1 3BH

www.hodderfaith.com

To my Mother and Father in gratitude for their early and abiding influence.

Acknowledgements

Mitch Albom, in *Tuesdays with Morrie*, was counselled by his much-loved Professor Morrie Schwartz that 'what makes a family is sticking together'.

In that regard I have been most blessed by a number of families who have stuck together around me and whose wise counsel and prayerful encouragement has been such an abiding support, comfort and reassurance to me over the years.

I dedicate *The Power of 3* to my mother, the lovely Jill Walker, who was indeed beautiful on the inside and on the outside and whose loving example of what it means to be a good person, mother and grandmother continues to inspire. I also dedicate this book to the memory of my father, Edwin Drummond, who despite his early death inspired this generation and the next with timeless words of unconditional love and exhortation to go on and have a go because, in his own words, 'You can do it!'

The lives and words of my mother and father inspired me in the setting up of Columba 1400 so that now thousands of young people of all ages have been inspired to discover their own inner greatness and so to have a go in life because they too have felt loved and treasured and believed in, perhaps for the very first time.

Going back to *Tuesdays with Morrie*, Professor Morrie Schwartz, knowing that he was dying, organised what he and Mitch Albom referred to as a 'living funeral' to thank all those who had been so kind to him in times past. If I could I would bring together over a 'family dinner of gratitude' Bill and Gina Christman, with whom I first worked in the gangland areas of Easterhouse in Glasgow; Colin and Helen Anderson, of the Old Kirk of West Pilton in

Edinburgh; Andrew and Irene McLellan, originally of Cartsburn Augustine Church in Greenock; David and Meg Ogston of Balerno Parish Church; Jim and Anne Lawson, as well as John and Elma Stuart, of St Andrew's Garrison Church in Aldershot; Dr Iain Gray, practical theologian extraordinaire; Professor Alec Cheyne, a supreme ecclesiastical historian; Professor Bill Shaw, whose love for life and for new possibilities made my transfer from a young aspiring lawyer to a minister possible; and Larry Parsons, who first recognised in me the vision that was to become Columba 1400. Alas, the sad loss of certain of these friends who have inspired me over the years has prevented such a get-together ever taking place – but I want to take this opportunity to express my heartfelt feelings of gratitude to them all.

I remain abidingly grateful to my incomparable literary agent, Kay McCauley, of the Pimlico Agency in New York, as indeed to Tom Farmer, Charlie Miller, Des Farmer and to Peter and Margaret Vardy, whose support and encouragement along the way has meant so much.

I also pay particular tribute to the indefatigable Wilma Shalliday, my outstanding assistant of many years at Loretto, Drummond International and at Columba 1400; and to my trusted and valued advisor Caro Handley, who have enabled the challenging experience of writing *The Power of 3* to be not only enjoyable but also exciting and inspiring. My personal debt to them is considerable.

Every effort has been made to source and gain permission to use material. My apologies if there are errors, which the publishers will endeavour to correct at the earliest opportunity.

If 'what makes a family is sticking together', then the entire Drummond family – now, with the happy and delightful arrival of Beau, expanding into a third generation – remains my 'rock'; to Elizabeth, Andrew and Rhona, Maggie and Mark and Beau, Marie Clare, Christian and Ruaraidh: thank you all for showing me the effectiveness of *The Power of 3* in your own lives.

Contents

The Journey Begins

This book began its life as a 'sensible' book. I intended to offer a calm and rational résumé of the compelling inner strength and power of Jesus of Nazareth. Drawing from the highs and lows of human life and expectation, I planned to write what theologians over the years have described as an 'apologia' for my simple yet deep belief in the story and teachings of Jesus.

And then something happened.

As the global recession swept in during the second half of 2008, the world around us changed, faster and more dramatically than any of us could have imagined. As the effects of the recession began to bite, high-street names disappeared, businesses – small and large – went under, people struggled to hold onto their homes, almost every family in the country cut back its spending, and young people who had worked hard for their qualifications were unable to find jobs.

There was a great deal of anxiety, uncertainty and fear. Throughout 2009, no one knew who might be next to lose their job, their home, their business, their income.

But amid all the grim consequences of recession, a profound change was happening. Not just the change in many people's material circumstances, but a widespread change in attitude. Suddenly 'things' did not matter so much and the focus began to change from the external – acquiring 'stuff' – to the internal, and the search for meaning in an increasingly uncertain world.

In the time of material prosperity which preceded the recession we thought we had all the answers. Money and possessions were what mattered most. Shopping had become an end, not a means – a way of feeling good and filling our homes and wardrobes with goodies that we then used to measure our worth and our success.

Even if we had our doubts, we believed that our political and financial leaders must know something we did not, so we put our trust in them. The invasion of Iraq, and its discredited claims that Iraq possessed weapons of mass destruction and could mobilise them to attack in forty-five minutes, followed by the massive global credit crisis, not to mention the scandal over British MPs' hugely inflated expense claims, put paid to such naïve thinking.

Instead people began to ask many more questions of those who lead and make decisions – and of themselves. Faced with issues that turned notions of right and wrong on their heads, and with financial and material uncertainty, many people have begun to ask what it really means to lead a good, decent and worthwhile life, what our true purpose is, and what we need to do to find inner satisfaction and peace.

In the words of Dr Jonathan Sacks, Chief Rabbi of the United Kingdom and the Commonwealth, 'It was only in the famines that the people of the Old Testament realised what the feasts were all about.' In other words, when things become tough, we begin to appreciate what really matters.

In my working life I come into contact with a great many people from all walks of life. As a former headmaster, a governor of two international schools and now a visiting Professor of Leadership in Education at Edinburgh University, I take a great interest in the lives of young people. I love seeing what paths former pupils have chosen to follow and never cease to be touched by the courage and determination I see in young people from all backgrounds.

In 1997 I fulfilled a long-held dream and set up Columba 1400, a purpose-built Community and International Leadership

Centre on the beautiful Isle of Skye off the west coast of Scotland. There we run leadership academies for youngsters from 'tough realities' – troubled backgrounds, broken homes, mean streets – and encourage them to believe in their own potential. Over the years since the Centre opened we have seen many wonderful, touching and inspiring stories emerge.

Columba 1400 is not just for the young or those from tough realities. It also offers leadership academies to teachers, educators, those in business – high achievers who want to step outside their daily lives and take a fresh look at the way they are living and working.

Our second Leadership Centre, on the banks of Loch Lomond, was officially opened by our patron, HRH The Princess Royal, in June 2010. Programmes based on the Columba 1400 model are also run in partnership with Activate Australia and Heartlines in South Africa.

While I am passionate about the work of Columba 1400, which is funded through many generous donations, I spend another portion of my week as a business coach within Drummond International, working in various parts of the world with individuals and groups across a wide range of organisations and addressing all kinds of issues.

Then there is my role as a chaplain and minister. This is the role that I love most, because it is a part of me that runs so deeply it underpins everything else I do. I worked as a young minister in the ganglands of Glasgow, then with the soldiers of the Parachute Regiment and The Black Watch. Today I am not employed by a specific church, group or neighbourhood, but will go where I am needed or invited.

In all these roles I come into contact with the old and the young, the rich and the poor, the ambitious and the modest, the driven and the uncertain. And increasingly those I meet, through my coaching work, through Columba 1400 and through my work as a minister, have a hunger for meaning and purpose in their lives and are asking the same questions:

- What is it that matters most to me?
- Where does the deepest satisfaction in life lie?
- How do I want to live my life?
- Is it time to step off the treadmill and find a new direction?
- And if so, to whom and to what shall I turn?

I believe that the answers to these questions are to be found in the life and example of Jesus of Nazareth. I am not a 'religious' type; I do not believe that we have to belong to one particular church or another, or that going to church makes you 'better' than those who do not; or even that you have to go to church at all in order to understand something of what it means to be spiritual. I suspect that the denomination someone belongs to is more a matter of 'where we land' than anything else. I have never agreed with religious leaders who take the attitude, 'We've got it right – and you haven't.' I happened to be born into a family who worshipped in the Church of Scotland, but to me the denomination matters far less than the spirit in which we live our beliefs. What makes sense to me, and always has, is Jesus, his life and his teachings: an extraordinary being, who spoke against opposing sects or groups, and who led by example. I feel that the lessons he taught are as richly relevant today, inspiring and comforting as when they were first given.

For some time I have been concerned and saddened by the way that the simple, down-to-earth goodness of the life of Jesus of Nazareth has so often come to be discarded and ignored by those who consider themselves to be 'rational'. It seems to me that to follow the example of someone with such a deep love for others, such natural wisdom and such selflessness, makes a great deal of sense.

The life and teachings of Jesus of Nazareth are as relevant and meaningful in the context of today's world as they have ever been. Yet Christianity, along with much else that is predominantly food for the spirit, has been discarded and pilloried. For some time now, the pervading attitude in our society has been that if you cannot feel it or touch it or prove it, then it cannot be real. Now I see evidence all around me that this is changing. Many people are growing weary of living with ambiguity, of the positioning of proof above all else, and of the spiritual emptiness that this way of thinking leaves in its wake.

In harsh times there can be few worse hardships than feeling that you are isolated and alone, neither understanding nor understood, and apparently powerless. We all have a deep longing to feel accepted, to belong, to know what we can rely on, and what a consistent set of tried and tested values might feel like.

This is the opportunity that emerges from a time of economic downturn. We have the chance to address afresh the fundamental questions of life and death, of good and evil, of life as we know it – and of life as it might yet become.

Jesus of Nazareth said, 'What good will it be for you to gain the whole world, yet forfeit your soul?' (Matt. 16:26). For too long we have neglected our souls, under the pressures of modern living – the 'to do' lists, the long working hours, the endless need to acquire more and do more. Now it is time to redress that balance and to recognise that without food for the soul, nothing else feels truly nourishing.

I believe that the time has come for a re-examination of our most fundamental principles. As the old Gaelic proverb says, 'In order to understand where you are going, it is very often necessary to remember where you have come from.' People everywhere are ready to ask, and to have answered, the deepest and most challenging questions of all. Rarely has there been such a significant time in modern history for ordinary men and women to stand up for and to publicly own what they believe in. Suddenly men and women of all faiths and none are newly aware of the need for values, and this is encouraging Christians to own their values fearlessly and stop apologising.

Why 'three'? Because as human beings we are made up of three parts – mind, body and spirit. And if we fail to address all three in equal measure we become like two-legged stools, wobbly and out of balance. So many of us have fed our bodies with nourishment and our minds with the food of intellect while neglecting our spirit and its equal need for sustenance.

Three is a hugely significant number, one which represents balance at the highest level of our being. Certainly for me, the answers to the most fundamental questions in life have also occurred in threes. Over time I have come to believe that there are three wisdoms, three principles and three qualities without which it is impossible to bring our spirit into balance with the rest of our being, to have a peaceful heart or to lead a fulfilling and worthwhile life.

In *The Power of Three* I will share these wisdoms, principles and qualities, in the hope that they will be of interest and value to you, as they have been to me.

The *Three Wisdoms* underpin every aspect of our lives and the way that we choose to live. The *Three Principles* will guide us and help us to lead lives of purpose and significance – not merely for ourselves and our families, but also for all those for whom we are responsible and who look to us for help or guidance. And the *Three Qualities* will, in their resonant timelessness, be more and more necessary in these times of challenge and opportunity. In a sense, these elements comprise what I like to think of as a spiritual 'tool-kit' which you can apply to any situation in your home life, work or relationships with others.

It is my hope that we will journey together through this book, as fellow travellers. Together we will look at the past, the present and the future. We will look at priorities and at possibilities and become brave and honest, with ourselves and with others – and in so doing we shall grow more deeply self-aware of who we really are, of what we might become and do with the rest of our life, drawing on the inspiration that comes from the life of Jesus and the ultimate three – the Trinity of Father, Son and Holy Spirit.

Jesus said, 'I have come that they may have life, and have it to the full' (John 10:10). That is what we all wish for: to live life to the full, and to discover the fullness, the richness, that there is in a life fully lived.

It is my hope that *The Power of Three* will enable the weary and the uncertain, as well as the person of faith, to discover their inner strength, to find purpose in life and explore their capacity for joy, and to see and believe in a new way forward.

The Three Wisdoms

For wisdom is more precious than rubies,
and nothing you desire can compare with her.

(Prov. 8:11)

The three wisdoms – *Serenity*, *Purpose* and *Service* – are so fundamental to a life lived with meaning that without them we are like buildings with no foundation, ready to topple if the wind blows too hard. We need these wisdoms to anchor us, to keep us grounded and to provide us with the courage and commitment to do what needs doing, even when the going gets tough.

The first wisdom is *Serenity*. This is a wisdom that rests primarily in the heart. When your heart is at ease and serene, your whole being is calm and centred. When your heart is filled with worry and fear, you become ill at ease and then ill in mind and body. You are no use to yourself or others, you make bad decisions and you lose your sense of joy in life. When your heart is serene, you have hope. You are able to wake up knowing you will find a way through whatever difficulties you face. Serenity brings inner peace; it allows us to listen fully to others and to our own inner guidance.

The second wisdom is *Purpose* which rests in the soul – the deep, inner life force that makes us human. Our purpose is rooted in our sense of direction in life. By this I do not mean ambition, but rather the direction that will bring us fulfilment and a feeling of completion, whatever that direction turns out to be. So many people are doing what they feel they ought to do, or what they have fallen into doing because there seemed no other choice. They have stepped onto a treadmill and do not know how to step off again. Find your sense of purpose, and choices will open up to you. Without purpose you are floundering, but with it the world becomes an exciting, meaningful place.

The final wisdom is *Service* and this rests in our very being. People need other people: we are not solitary creatures. Yet if we are with others only in a selfish, dominant and arrogant way, there is no happiness to be found, no sense of connection, either within ourselves or with them. When we bring a sense of service, then we find a deep sense of joy in being able to help, guide, restore and care for those around us.

When we live our lives according to these three wisdoms, we live with understanding, knowing that there will always be a path to follow and that inner guidance and trust will lead us towards it.

Serenity

Do not lose your inward peace for anything
whatsoever, even if your whole world seems upset.

(St Francis de Sales)

No search is more pressing, in our world today, than the search for serenity.

Think of how many people you know, young and not so young, rich and not so rich, happy and not so happy, who are rushing through life. We are all at it – racing to catch up with ourselves, doing two or three things at once, cutting down on sleep in order to squeeze everything into our day, and always feeling that there is never enough time.

Such has become the frenetic pace of modern living, of working and of earning, of buying and of getting, that very few of us have real quality time for ourselves and our families, time for being rather than doing.

Most of the gadgets intended to make life easier appear to have done just the opposite. Emails have added another chore to our daily list and yet somehow, it seems, we still need to make the same number of phone calls and write the same number of letters as we did before the World Wide Web came along. Our homes are filled with time-saving gadgets that somehow do not save us time at all. Or perhaps we just find extra tasks to fill in any time that actually is saved.

Lack of sleep, stress and overwork are making many of us ill, but being unwell is no longer always a good enough excuse for a rest. In a recent survey on the quality of working life, based on the views of over 1,500 managers, almost half felt that illness rates in their organisations were rising, while one in three claimed that employees in their organisation were expected to work while sick.

We all know that when we are tired, we make mistakes. In 2008 there were over 4,000 avoidable mistakes made in Britain's hospitals by overworked, overtired medical staff who, in a blur of exhaustion, misdiagnosed ailments, operated on the wrong parts of patients or prescribed the wrong treatment, sometimes with tragic consequences.[1]

It is not just in the Western economies that the impact of this overwork culture is being felt; it is rebounding around the world. For instance, in India, where the economy is growing rapidly, the boom may have brought spiralling corporate profits, but rates of heart disease, strokes and diabetes – all previously very low – are soaring.

Overwork can kill. In 2008 a junior doctor in Britain died after working excessive hours and sleeping very little; in Japan a man killed himself recently after working for seventeen months without a day off; and in France it was reported that twenty-five employees of the corporate giant France Telecom company committed suicide during 2008 and the early part of 2009.

While all this overwork is going on, the joys of family life are being lost. For instance, what could be more wonderful than the birth of a baby? In Britain fathers are now entitled to two weeks paid paternity leave and a further thirteen weeks unpaid, an advance in working conditions that few actually take advantage of, citing their fear of losing their jobs, harming their career prospects or looking as though they are not committed enough. So commitment to family gives way to commitment to work and everyone – except perhaps the corporate profiteers – loses.

The great economist John Maynard Keynes wrote in 1928, 'Let us for the sake of argument suppose that a hundred years from now we are eight times better off in the economic sense than we are today.' He was close: the gross domestic profit in the United States is today 6.5 times larger than in 1928 and growing, and the situation in Britain is not dissimilar. But Keynes also believed that with this growing economic wealth, we would have a growing amount of leisure time. He believed that by this stage we would be working two hours a day and the problem would be how to use our spare time. For a few decades after he wrote this, people did seem to be working fewer hours, as more were entitled to paid holidays and annual leave. But since 1985 we in Britain and in the United States – two of the world's leading economies – have been putting in increasingly long hours. Today full-time workers in Britain work the longest hours in Europe, averaging 43.6 per week compared to an average of 40.3 in the European Union.

This extract from an article by former *Observer* political editor Gaby Hinsliff, writing in the autumn of 2009 about her decision to resign, sums it up so well:

> Every day became a battle against the clock. I never listened properly to phone conversations with friends, because I was always simultaneously doing something else. I was so on edge I raged at the tiniest delay – tourists blocking tube escalators, a computer slow to spark up in the morning. Running for the train in high heels, I sprained my ankle; the doctor prescribed some exercises but who had time for that? I wore flat shoes, took painkillers.
>
> My reward was that for two crazed but fantastic years, I did – in that loaded cliché – have it all: terrific job, plus small child . . . but what got lost in the rush was a life, if a life means having time for the people you love, engaging with the world around you, making a home rather than just running a household.[2]

So what is going on? Why are we better off than our predecessors (even in times of recession) but working harder? Has a culture of overwork blinded us to the fact that we need not work such long hours? Many experts believe this to be the case. Overwork has become part of our culture. There are tyrannical bosses, of course, but mostly we work because we tell ourselves we have to, and as a result we are all willing slaves, endangering our health, relationships and happiness for the sake of clocking up hours. We drive ourselves, having come to believe that more is better – more work, more acquisition, more demands on ourselves – until eventually we begin to feel out of control. We are helpless, and yet longing to find a way to stop, rest and simplify our lives.

Of course some people love their jobs, and would not change a thing. But this is not true for most. The vast majority of people – 87 per cent, a recent survey found – would give up work tomorrow if they could afford to. Another survey reported that three-quarters of their respondents would like to cut their hours, and another that half of all working mothers would rather stay at home with their children.

When Gaby Hinsliff resigned from her job, she was astonished by the reaction of those around her:

> I never expected the emotional outpouring that followed. 'Wish I had the guts to do the same,' texted a junior minister. A seemingly unflappable public relations executive confessed secretly agonising over 'not being the kind of mother my son deserves'; a colleague whose slick work-life balance I had always envied admitted she was 'at the end of my tether', dying to quit.
>
> Confessions tumbled compulsively from people I barely knew: tales of stricken marriages, miscarriages, only children who were meant to have siblings but then a career got in the way. 'Too many of us once had relationships that we haven't got now because of this job,' said a veteran male reporter.[3]

When we live life at a frenetic pace, the balance of our lives suffers. It becomes impossible to balance the needs of work, leisure, family and friends, just as it is impossible to balance our mind, body and spirit.

We are three-dimensional beings, and all of our dimensions need equal care. Unless this happens we simply cannot create balance in our lives. To find outer balance, we must first create inner balance.

It is easier to see to the outer physical needs of our lives than it is to attend to the deeper, if not more essential, inner needs. Yet these inner needs – for reflection, serenity, internal dialogue and spiritual sustenance – do not disappear when they are ignored. Rather, they nag away at us, manifesting in a sense of discontent and emptiness, a feeling that 'something is missing', or even developing into depression, which, according to the World Health Organisation, is dramatically on the increase.

Inwardly perplexed, we look for quick-fix solutions: a new outfit or car, a holiday, a promotion, a night out. There is nothing wrong with these things; they can all be wonderfully cheering and fun. But if we do not address our true inner needs, these outer fixes are like tipping a glass of water into a bucket with a hole in it – they simply do not work.

There is a choice

When life feels hectic and driven, it is easy to feel that there is no choice. But whatever our circumstances, we always have a choice. We can remain in the hustle and bustle, throw ourselves into another argument, dive into another drink, buy another dress or shirt – or we can decide to step back and take a good look at our lives and our habits and begin to make changes.

Mark was an outwardly successful executive in a grow-ing company. Married with two small children, he worked a twelve-hour day and saw his children only at weekends – if he wasn't racing into the office to do a bit more overtime. When he walked into my office for a consultation he was grey and drawn, with shadows under his eyes and tightness in his jaw. 'I feel stuck,' he told me. 'I love my job, but it's taking over my life. I'm exhausted, I hardly ever see my kids, my wife is lonely and I'm running myself into the ground trying to keep my demanding boss happy. I don't want to leave my job, but what else can I do?'

Mark was typical of some of the bright, successful men and women who come through my door looking for answers. They are talented and full of energy and ambition, and while they are not looking for a complete change in lifestyle, their lives are out of balance and work-driven and they are apparently always in an agitated, anxious and adrenalised state. Like so many others, Mark was looking outside himself for a 'solution'. But no lasting solution is going to be found until we look inwards and make the connection between our heads and our hearts.

At a recent appearance, the Dalai Lama, the spiritual leader of Tibet, was asked what solutions he had for the problems of society – local, national and international.

He replied, 'We are always looking to them out there: to others, to governments, to solve things. The real answer is you.'

And then, pointing to his heart and to the hearts of the large gathering before him, he said again and again, 'In here, in here, in your heart . . . and mine.'

The Dalai Lama exudes calm, centred serenity. He also laughs a great deal, and clearly enjoys himself when he talks to other people. His serenity is infectious; it draws others to him, whether or not they are Buddhists.

But it is not only spiritual or religious leaders who can exude serenity. Many people manage it. We can all think of people we know who appear calm in the eye of a storm, who are clear-headed and never seem to panic, who appear to know something those around them do not. And when we come across a person like this, we are usually intrigued and wish to know more. How can we be like them? How do they manage it?

Some time ago I was invited to Mumbai in India to advise on the setting up of an international school. My host was the patron of the school, a wealthy Indian man who had made a great deal of money. On meeting him I was immediately struck by his warmth and his calm manner. Over the next few days, as we worked together and talked, I learned that he had made the decision to change his life and live for others. He no longer lived extravagantly, as he once had; now he wore a simple white garment, walked everywhere and never carried more than twenty dollars on him. In the words of his revered Mahatma 'Great Soul' Gandhi he had made the decision, he told me, to 'become the change you want to see'. He put his money, his time and his energy into creating projects to help others, and into bringing people together in shared purpose.

I noticed that this Hindu father had two sons, both of whom were married to Muslim women. Yet this appeared to present few problems, so I asked him how, in such a divided country, he managed to hold together a family divided across faiths. He turned to me and said, 'In your countries in the West you do "learning" very well. But in my country, here in the East, we also do "wisdom".' Then he laughed and told me that he loved both his daughters-in-law dearly, and never saw faith as a reason to be divided.

Like my Indian friend, those who have decided what is most important to them, and exude the joy that follows from it, have made an active choice. They have chosen to take the time to look inwards, and to follow a path that fills their hearts with serenity. This is not a simple choice, nor always an easy one, but it leads to great rewards. Few things are more precious than peace of mind, inner calm and a sense that all is well with your world.

Look within

To whom shall we turn in our search for this deep inner wisdom of serenity? Today there are all sorts of helpful people and agencies who are there to listen and to prescribe. Yet while they can often be supportive with particular problems, so often these interventions are transitory and the bleakness and sense of being alone with our problems returns.

This is why, to find a lasting and accessible sense of serenity, we need to turn inwards, making the most of our own resources and reaching towards the lasting love and support of God.

Jesus of Nazareth said, 'The kingdom of God [or heaven] is within you' (Luke 17:21 NIV). We all have the opportunity of finding heaven on this earth if we are willing to work at finding the inner stillness which allows us to connect with ourselves and to know God.

When Jesus told those around him to look within to find the kingdom of heaven, his words would have been radical. For this bright, attractive and unusual young teacher, with his growing following, to question the norms of his day was unthinkable to many. For the huge majority, the answers to significant life questions lay in scrolls, heavy and precious tomes over which wise men pored. Their interpretation of what was written was considered final, and sadly contained many more 'thou shalt nots' than 'why nots'.

Then Jesus came along and literally turned things upside down. We must stop blaming others or always looking to others for solutions, he said. We must stop the 'impossibility talk', give up on our 'woe is me' attitudes, and begin thinking of the possible and of the 'why not?' perspective.

Such revolutionary thinking turned the Jewish world view upside down and for many it was more than a step too far.

Yet others – those for whom the Law was oppressive and just too hard – found it liberating and encouraging. For them it was enlightenment itself to know that life and faith, purpose and significance were not dependent on a distant and at times despotic God. Here in human flesh was someone who spoke of another way of being and a better way of knowing God. In the teaching of Jesus of Nazareth there was an enhanced sense of the partnership between the human and the divine. No wonder people said after hearing him, 'No one has ever spoken like this man.'

So what of the here and now in your life? How do we apply the extraordinary lessons that Jesus taught – and that so many others since have repeated, in one form or another?

Are you ready to claim or to reclaim the spiritual part, the true essence, the third dimension of your life and of your inner being? If you are, then we will need to examine, from the inside out as well as from the outside in, what it means to be serene in heart.

The first thing I tell those who come to me, like Mark, looking for advice, is that if they seriously want to be calmer, quieter in body and soul, they first need to realise that they have to work at it. This may sound like a contradiction, since they are already working so hard and would like to ease this burden, but in order to make a change in their way of being and doing, effort is required.

Frère Roger, founder of the world-famous ecumenical monastic community in Taizé, France, which welcomes those of all faiths and persuasions, said, 'Nothing good comes without an element of struggle.'

Step out of the darkness

Jesus said to his followers:

> Your eye is the lamp of your body. When your eyes are healthy, your whole body also is full of light. But when they are unhealthy, your body also is full of darkness. See to it, then, that the light within you is not darkness. Therefore, if your whole body is full of light, and no part of it dark, it will be just as full of light as when a lamp shines its light on you. (Luke 11:34–36)

The darkness of our past, our thoughts and deeds, our mistakes and hurts to ourselves and to others can overwhelm us. All of these have a curious way of burdening us and making us dark inside.

What darkness do you hold deep inside? Perhaps you have old hurts which have not healed. Perhaps as a child you were abused, either physically or mentally, or suffered a loss you have never fully dealt with. Perhaps it is only now that you can begin to make sense of what happened.

Or perhaps there are difficulties in your life right now. Perhaps your husband or wife or partner is planning to leave you; perhaps you are deeply worried about the direction in which another person is going in his or her life. If you are worried about someone else, you may long to be able to help them, yet be unable to muster the calmness of mind that will enable you to make sense of what is happening so that you can be there for them. After all, how can you possibly be of any use to them if your own inner life is in turmoil?

It may be, also, that you are worried about aspects of your own behaviour. Are you impatient, critical, judgemental? Are you less than honest in your dealings, or dismissive of the feelings and needs of others?

If so, then it is time to take a good look at yourself in the mirror. Do your eyes reflect inner serenity, or turmoil?

In this 'mirror-gazing' experience we have to begin to take hold of our own lives – or, even better, surrender them in their entirety to our higher spiritual power, to God as we know him through the physical expression of the life, stories and wisdom of Jesus of Nazareth.

Forgive

Jesus managed to sustain serenity in his heart through the worst the world could throw against him.

Imagine how it must have felt for him to be 'tracked' by the religious authorities in his every word and action. It was, in some ways, a forerunner of modern multimedia exposure (possibly even worse, bearing in mind the surprising efficacy of the oral tradition of his day). Few could read or write, but they could talk and listen and retell stories, and everyone in that chain would feel a personal engagement. A well-placed whisper in a dark alley could rapidly become a 'truth' relayed in the light of day in the marketplace. 'See the people with whom he is speaking and associating,' they would say. 'He spends time with the tax-gatherers and prostitutes and sinners.'

Choosing to break with all convention, he even spent time talking at a well with a Samaritan woman. The Samaritans and their practices were at odds with those of the Jewish people, and no self-respecting Jewish man would talk to a strange woman in public.

Imagine the reaction, too, when he chose not to condemn the woman found in adultery, to whom he said, 'Go now and leave your life of sin.' Turning to the crowd, he said, 'Let any one of you who is without sin be the first to throw a stone at her' (John 8:7–11).

This was extraordinary to most people then. The impact of what Jesus said and did caused many people seriously to question their own inherited and accepted attitudes. His calm assurance encouraged discussion and dialogue. The lives of those earliest disciples were full of struggle, not unlike yours and mine. They too had their doubts, fears and uncertainties. They too had to face good times and bad. And they too were looking for a spiritual presence that would enable them to feel calmer inside and to discover the wisdom of serenity. Imagine them talking among themselves: 'How much I would love to be like that. He seems so real, so full of life and love and so assured of who he is and what life is all about. . .'

But there were also those who feared and distrusted what he said because they did not understand it, chief among them the authorities of the day, who condemned him outright. Even in the midst of his own suffering, he reached out with the message, 'No matter what has been, no matter how desperate you are feeling, no matter how unsure you are of yourself or others, I am with you at all times. I love you and forgive you so much that the first thing you need to be able to do is to learn to forgive yourself.'

We all make, and will surely continue to make, mistakes from which we will long to be forgiven and to recover. And we have all been hurt by the actions of other people. But when you begin to learn to forgive yourself and others, you are stepping back out onto the right road towards finding serenity in your heart and the contentment and joy of knowing God. From this sense of his presence, his forgiveness and his love will come an inner wisdom which draws from all your previous experiences and so allows you to feel serene in your heart.

While I was being driven to a speaking engagement in the United States, I began to feel distinctly nervous and unsure of myself. The car stopped at a set of traffic lights and I looked to my left to see a church whose wayside pulpit read, 'God loves you . . . no matter what.' It was the message I needed, and from that moment on I began to relax and to trust that everything would go well.

It is a wonderful thing to know that we are never truly alone. And it is that deep love and forgiveness that enables us, to paraphrase the words of the writer to the Philippians, to 'forget what is behind and press forward to what lies ahead' (see Phil. 3:13–14).

Forgiveness is an extraordinary thing. It allows space in our hearts for peace and serenity, and the more serene we are in our hearts the less likely we are to repeat our mistakes.

Ask yourself, who do you need to forgive in your life? What do you need to forgive yourself for? Is there someone to whom you need to say sorry, or to make amends?

Self-acceptance, letting go of the past, believing the promises of God's love and forgiveness – if we can do all these things they will indeed enable us to 'Be still, and know . . . God' (Ps. 46:10) and perhaps better understand how those earliest disciples must have felt when Jesus said to them, 'Peace I leave with you; my peace I give you. I do not give to you as the world gives. Do not let your hearts be troubled and do not be afraid' (John 14:27).

Spend time alone

In order to let go of any inner 'darkness', to learn to forgive yourself and others and to find serenity in your heart, you need to find a way, in an already busy life, to create a time of space and peace.

Jesus spent a great deal of time on his own, perhaps far more time than commentators or the stories suggest to our reading. But there are references enough to how he would quietly and calmly withdraw, no doubt reflecting on the words of Isaiah, 'You will keep in perfect peace those whose minds are steadfast, because they trust in you' (Isa. 26:3).

This regular withdrawal to listen, to be quiet and to pray was a hallmark of Jesus' life and ministry. Indeed, he urged his disciples, 'Come with me by yourselves to a quiet place and get some rest' (Mark 6:31).

I firmly believe that no person of real lasting goodness and significance can get by without such a practice. I often wonder how statesmen or politicians can sustain any form of integrity of mind and purpose given the relentless media-driven '24-hour response' pressure of their public lives. How can you constantly 'be there' for others if you never have any time for yourself?

How much time are you giving to yourself to be at peace, to breathe deeply and to sit quietly, pausing in your day and deciding not to allow the pressures you face to trouble your heart? To develop a regular practice of quiet time spent alone is the most valuable stepping stone there is to inner peace and serenity.

Here is an exercise which can be enormously helpful.

Sit in a quiet place with a pen and paper and think about the following questions: *How do you distract yourself from being simply with yourself? What stops you spending ten or fifteen minutes just 'doing nothing'?*

Make a list of all the things that distract you. This might include television, browsing on the computer, reading a newspaper, talking on the phone, housework, paperwork, focusing on others, making something to eat and so on. We all have a thousand and one distractions.

Now think of a place, or an activity, in which you have felt connected to yourself – in other words, when you were able to engage all of yourself in what you were doing. This might be gardening, walking somewhere beautiful, soaking in a warm bath, or doing something creative, like painting.

Now think about how you experienced your own self at that time – perhaps you felt softer, more relaxed, more at ease and open.

It may be a while since you have done any of these things, but still, remember the sense of calm and connection that you felt while totally absorbed.

Remembering this is valuable, for it shows you what is possible, and now that you know there has been a time when you felt calm and connected, you can work to re-create this and expand it, either by repeating the activity, or just by dwelling on the feelings that went with it.

Or try this second exercise.

Seek out a quiet place, somewhere away from all distractions, where you can be still. This might be a room in your home, a quiet corner in your garden, or a favourite bench in the spot where you walk your dog. All that matters is that it is somewhere you like to be, and that there is no interruption, loud noise or obvious distraction.

Sit quietly for a few minutes and in the silence allow your mind to be still and calm. This takes practice. Calming the mind can bring up resistance, in the form of inner chatter – a succession of thoughts and concerns. Do not worry about this, just inwardly take a step back from it and, without judging, notice how busy your mind is. As each new thought arrives, let it go without examining it.

Make this exercise a daily practice, or if you cannot manage every day, as often as you are able. Try to do it at the same time each day, so that this small segment of time becomes yours, a special time in which you are simply yourself.

As you become more used to letting your 'mind chatter' go, you will begin to feel a sense of space and peace. It is in this space that you will be able to make sense of where you have come from and the burdens you have been carrying, to admit to any sense of loneliness as well as the pain of any guilt and disappointment in yourself or others.

Be prepared also that in the silence you may find that tears flow. Let the tears come; it is all part of inner cleansing. The washing of our eyes with tears is our heart's way of telling our heads that it is time to get sorted out and to begin again.

It is in these moments of still reflection that we are able to see more clearly and to find the answers we seek. This is a time to begin asking the fundamental questions:

• Where am I going – and what might I yet become?
• What, and who, matters most to me?

Connect with the divine

This quiet time might also be a chance to reflect on the power of the divine, a wonderful opportunity to open your heart to God, even if he is as yet either unknown or unrecognised by you. For each one of us in the search for the wisdom of serenity has it within us to 'be still and know God'. The much loved Irish Celtic writer John O'Donoghue described God as 'the unfillable hole in our lives'.

Down through history various routes to God have been earnestly espoused – even within Christianity. The study of theology, faith and practice, doing good works, committing to a purpose and getting on with it, being there for others, going about and doing good are all cited, and may all be valid. Yet none of these is as central or important as getting right inwardly with yourself and so beginning to fill in the 'unfillable hole' that we come to know as God.

There may seem to be many apparently unfillable holes in your life. All of us have them and we seek to fill them in many different ways.

Often the deepest 'unfillable hole' for most of us is that we do not really like ourselves, who or what we have become. In fact you may have been so busy trying to be someone or something that you are not that you have fundamentally lost sight of who you are and who you are meant to be.

Some years ago I received a request to lead a retreat for a group of overworked, high-flying business men and women at Pluscarden Abbey, the Benedictine monastery near Elgin in the north of Scotland.

At the introductory session, when our host monk asked if there were any questions, one man asked, 'What is your five-year plan?' The monk smiled warmly and said, 'There isn't one, other than to pray and live and be there for others.' Another of the visiting group asked, 'Where will you be in a year's time?' to which the monk replied, 'Here!'

These rather thoughtless and arrogant questions in no way fazed the monks. And over the following couple of days the rich, steady, calm self-discipline of their lives so impressed the visitors that at the end of our stay apologies were made and more than one of the visitors said to the monks, 'If only we had your serenity of heart!'

Yet however much those business people may have come to admire the quiet life and discipline of those Benedictine monks, there was no way that was going to be the life for them. For most of us, our lives have been set or chosen and we find ourselves in very different circumstances, a far cry from calm monasticism. Because of this we have to find our own ways to create the still, calm spaces in which we can find a connection with ourselves and with God and regain sight of who we truly are, the diamond at the core, shedding the dark outer layers of thoughtlessness, arrogance and narrow-mindedness.

So close your eyes and visualise the surrounding presence and power of the Holy Spirit, who longs to calm you and to still your heart. In practising this during your quiet moments, you will reset your compass and find clarity in thought, understanding and direction.

Serenity with others

If the starting point is to learn to cultivate serenity while you are alone, then the next step is to learn to maintain that serenity in the company of others.

For Jesus, one followed the other. In order to be serene, and so to be fully present for and among others, he knew that he had to have time to himself, by himself, in quiet reflection and with his Father in prayer.

If they had existed at the time, the tabloid newspapers of the day might easily have been filled with headlines proclaiming 'Critics confounded by Jesus' energy', 'Supernatural powers of recovery'.

But for him, as so often for all of us, these personal withdrawals did not always go according to plan. For example, when, at the end of a long hot day, just as the disciples were looking forward to some rest and a meal, they discovered a huge crowd waiting to hear Jesus speak, the disciples urged him to send the crowd home. Yet Jesus, who must have been the most tired of them all, remained serene. He had compassion towards the huge crowd, for they were 'like sheep without a shepherd' (Matt. 9:36). And so began what history now recalls as the 'feeding of the five thousand', which might never have taken place had Jesus not demonstrated such serenity of heart in difficult and unexpected circumstances. His regular time of prayer, on his own, enabled him to draw deeply on his spiritual reserves, thereby enabling him to remain calm when needed, and to ensure that a massive crowd was listened to and heard and fed.

What Jesus taught us was that serenity of heart in times of crisis is expressed not in what we say, but in *who* and *how* we are in those circumstances. For the person who is serene in heart, there can and should be no need for fine words, practised lines or rehearsed gestures. A serene heart, established during your times of quiet reflection and spiritual connection, will enable you to live in the moment and to trust your instincts and judgements.

There may be moments when others, perhaps unexpectedly, look to you for a lead. It is then that you are into 'deep breath country', when, rather like a swan's feet, your mind may be paddling rapidly below the surface, but your outer feathers need to remain calm so you can appear to glide effortlessly along.

Do not be afraid to take your time within a group setting: you could take the lead and ask for a few minutes of silence. Encourage those gathered with you to listen to one another and share knowledge, rather than challenging each other with the superiority of their own ideas.

The strangest and most lovely thing about practising the wisdom of serenity, either on your own or collectively, is that you can and do become better at it! The visualisation of the accompanying presence of Jesus of Nazareth and his Holy Spirit will guide, encourage and sustain you 'no matter what'. And with that knowledge we can perhaps more easily accept that there is no such thing as perfection in this life, and that it is 'OK to be OK'.

Reflections

When you cannot physically go to the quiet place that is special or holy to you, visualise it in your mind. Breathe deeply and allow yourself to rest there for a few moments, and if you can, to feel the accompanying presence of Jesus of Nazareth, in order to renew your energy and keep your heart filled with serenity.

If you know that you want to make changes in your life – large or small – but feel unsure about where to start, then begin by changing one habit. For instance, walk instead of driving, eat lunch in the park instead of at your desk, get up half an hour earlier in order to be less rushed, phone the person you love when they least expect it, or switch off the television and listen to inspiring music instead.

When entering a room or a new situation, take your time, breathe deeply and walk more slowly than usual. Try not to rush in your words and movements and so allow others to feel quieter and more comfortable around you. Allow peace to take the place of panic and considered decision-making to take the place of mindless reaction to pressing circumstances.

Purpose

God speaks in the silence
and only those who are quiet can hear what he says.

(Inscription above to the entrace to Pluscarden Abbey)

If the wisdom of serenity helps us look into our hearts and discover who we really are, then the wisdom of purpose enables us to work out why we are here. For every one of us there is a path along which we can travel with unwavering direction and purpose, no matter how great the obstacles. To find that path and to travel it brings meaning to our lives and is the source of a deep and lasting sense of joy.

A great many people are spending their lives doing something that does not inspire, encourage or even interest them. They get up, go to work, get through the day, whether pleasantly or unpleasantly, and then go home. They are denied the satisfaction that comes from feeling that there is nothing they would rather have spent their day doing. Aware that they would rather be somewhere else, doing something else, they wait and hope for something better to turn up, but settle for more of the same if it does not.

All too often the sense of disappointment and frustration that inevitably results is numbed through exciting but ultimately unrewarding activities like partying, drug-taking, drinking too much, pursuing extreme sports, overspending or looking for excitement in the form of a new home, a new relationship or a new job. A great deal of effort can be put into avoiding having to find the answer to the question, 'Why am I here?'

Those who come through my door for a consultation often tell me they are looking for meaning in their lives. In many cases something – perhaps a moment of crisis – has caused them to pause and ask searching questions about what they really want to do with their lives. It is like going on a journey, then stopping for a rest and realising that you do not know where the journey is leading. How can you feel directed and inspired if you do not know where you are going?

> 'I feel driven to do something,' one young woman told me recently. 'I just don't know what it is.'
> 'That's a great place to start,' I told her. 'You've already taken the first step; you know there's something out there for you. Now you have to find out what it is.'

Sadly, in this media- and celebrity-driven age, a lot of young people (and some not so young) decide that their purpose is to be rich, or famous, or both. But while this may be an exciting goal, it is nothing to do with real purpose. If you discover that your true purpose is to sing, you feel passionate about singing and put all your heart and effort into it and then it happens to make you very successful, well then, that is wonderful. There are those who follow their true purpose, whether that is to sing, to write, to paint, to work in medicine or science or government, and who in doing so find great success. But this success will always be secondary, an unexpected benefit, rather than the actual purpose.

Nobel prize-winning scientists, doctors and writers do not set out to win a Nobel prize, they set out to investigate, experiment, heal, advance knowledge or write the best book they are capable of, whether or not it brings them public acknowledgement, riches or fame.

True purpose is rooted in the soul. But what is the soul? The closest I can come to describing it is that deep inner life force at our very core, the essence of us that is wise and sees truth, the deepest, most genuine part of us. To discover your soul is to learn what it means to be truly human and fully alive, to realise your inner strength, to discover your spiritual wings – and your true potential.

Jesus said, 'What good will it be for you to gain the whole world, yet forfeit your soul?' (Matt. 16:26). He meant that no amount of riches or outer success can compensate if you are not connected to your soul and its true purpose.

We all have the potential to do extraordinary things when we have a deep and profound sense of purpose. And for each of us that purpose is different.

The first time I had a sense of what my purpose in life might be, I was in Sunday school. Our teacher, Mrs Roy, told us the story of the Good Samaritan. As she told us the tale that Jesus had told – of a Jew attacked by bandits and left for dead, ignored by the priest and the Levite who passed by on the other side, and of the despised Samaritan who helped the man, bathed his wounds and took him to an inn, where he paid for his care – I listened, spellbound. Here, in this simple yet powerful story, was something that made perfect sense to me. The lights came on for me, and I knew that I wanted to be the kind of person who would do as that Samaritan did.

The sense of purpose that dawned in me that day has never left me. I haven't always found it easy to follow, but it has continued to be my guiding light in life.

Years after that Sunday school lesson, when I had completed my law degree at Cambridge University, I had the opportunity to spend the summer working for a very smart, well-respected law firm in my home town. My mother was delighted: she hoped they would offer me a permanent position and that I would go on to be a successful lawyer. One day, one of the senior partners in the firm went out to lunch and asked me to take a precognition statement from a client. I spent the next two hours with a nervous young woman who wanted a divorce, taking down the details of her husband's mistreatment of her.

While she was speaking I realised, in a moment of absolute clarity, that I didn't want to be here in an office, helping to dismantle her marriage. I wanted to become part of her story much earlier. I wanted to get involved with people's lives in a way I would never be able to do as a lawyer, offering help, support, advice and encouragement. The passion I had felt as a small boy of seven, listening to the story of the Good Samaritan, resurfaced and I knew, once again, my true purpose.

After that summer I turned away from the law and went into the Church, working in a Glasgow inner-city parish where I was able to make the kind of contribution that felt real and meaningful to me. My decision meant letting my mother down, which wasn't easy, but it taught me that sometimes, in order to follow your purpose, you are going to have to disappoint others.

I was very lucky to have discovered my sense of purpose early on in life. For some of us, our purpose is right under our noses, while for others, finding it is a more complex business. When that is the case, the temptation is to cling onto something, anything. 'I'll feel better when I get that promotion,' people say, or, 'I think I'll be happier when we move,' or, 'I'm going to try a completely different job.' There is nothing wrong with any of these things, as long as they are what the person truly wants to do and not simply a way of passing time and filling in the blanks left by an absence of purpose. Without a sense of purpose we can often feel empty, directionless and unmotivated.

So how do you find your purpose in life? The first clue is that it will be part of the essence of you, something that fits with who you truly are and with your beliefs and principles in life. And it will be something that benefits mankind. I do not necessarily mean working directly for the good of others, though it may involve this, but it will be something that, in the overall scheme of things, is a good thing for humanity. It might be on a grand scale – pushing back frontiers of medicine or exploration, for example. Or it might be – as is the case for most of us – very simple and ordinary. You might be drawn to teach others, to shape new laws or enforce those that already exist, to excel physically through dance or sport, to act or sing, giving pleasure to an audience, to cook delicious food or to design beautiful homes. The key thing is that our real purpose will never work to harm or hurt others, and will, ultimately, always be good for us and for those around us.

Not everyone will find or fulfil their purpose in their working lives. It may be that what you do away from your job is what matters most deeply to you. For some this starts out as voluntary work or a hobby which becomes more and more central in their life, and in the end they find a way to make it their main occupation. When you find your purpose, you want to follow it all the time: you feel passionate about it. Purpose engenders passion. And what is wonderful is that we are all so different. James Dyson felt passionate about inventing a new kind of vacuum cleaner. Jamie Oliver felt passionate about feeding children healthy food. Ellen MacArthur felt passionate about sailing. David Attenborough felt passionate about exploring and showing people the wonders of the animal kingdom.

There are those who might protest that life is simply for having fun – eat, drink and be merry, and let's not worry about anything else. But they are missing something vital: to be without purpose is merely to *exist* rather than truly to *live*. Purpose is about fulfilling our true potential, stretching ourselves, daring to try, working our socks off to achieve, having a go and then having another go when it all goes wrong, getting back up after every setback and making our hopes and dreams come true.

So what is your purpose?

Begin today

If you feel that you have no idea, or perhaps only a vague idea, of what your purpose might be, then begin by appreciating all that you have and all that is good in your world. Open yourself up to the possibilities around you. In this way you recognise and appreciate what is of value to you and you can begin to recognise and appreciate your own potential.

The Dalai Lama puts it beautifully when he says:

> Every day, think as you wake up, today I am fortunate to have woken up, I am alive, I have a precious human life, I am not going to waste it. I am going to use all my energies to develop myself. To expand my heart out to others, to achieve enlightenment for the benefit of all beings, I am going to have kind thoughts towards others, I am not going to get angry or think badly about others, I am going to benefit others as much as I can.[1]

There is a simplicity, a genuineness, a delightful light touch in the Dalai Lama's teachings that makes them enormously attractive and accessible. Thousands – people of all faiths and of none – gather to hear him speak as he travels around the world. He states simple truths which go straight to the heart. So in the serenity of your heart, nurture warm and loving thoughts, gratitude and goodwill, and then ask yourself this:

• If I did know what my purpose was, what would it be?

This question asks you to take a leap of faith. Do not think before answering, just say whatever comes into your head – you just might surprise yourself. And remember that the realisation of our true direction does not necessarily come in the big moments or the grand gestures. Rather, it is often in the quietest of moments and the gentlest of gestures that we find our true life's purpose.

Step out of the drawer

There is an old Danish proverb which runs, 'It is difficult to open the drawer when you are inside.' Sometimes we can hole up inside our internal mental drawers and find it far too difficult to open up and look outside our immediate lives to see just what might be possible.

We all need to 'step out of the drawer' sometimes, to look from the outside at ourselves and our lives. Hence the overriding importance of spending quiet time alone, practising and embracing the wisdom of serenity. It is during quiet, reflective periods of time that we can see ourselves more clearly.

Sometimes stepping out of the drawer can be frightening. What will you find? What might be asked of you? Will you be up to the challenges you set for yourself, or will you let yourself and others down?

When we research the lives of great men and women, not least in the Bible, we find many perplexed and agonised souls who were for the most part scared rigid at the prospect of what might be asked of them.

Nowhere do we have a more vivid picture of this than when Jesus was facing his ultimate test in the Garden of Gethsemane. In the throes of his humanity he was driven to pray, 'Father, if it is possible, may this cup be taken from me' (Matt.26:39). Some weeks earlier he had set his face towards Jerusalem, knowing that he had to do what he had to do for a higher, nobler purpose. No wonder that commentators have said that Jesus was at his most courageous and victorious the night before he died.

There was a purposeful fire burning within Jesus' heart, an unquenchable flame. And many others have felt such a flame in their own hearts. For Moses, the Old Testament tells us, this took the form of a visible burning bush. So do not be afraid to 'step out of the drawer' and discover what it is that fills you with passion or sets you alight.

Remember, too, if you feel uncertain or fearful, that we are all part of God's greater purpose.

When Jesus said, 'The kingdom of God [or heaven] is within you' (Luke 17:21 NIV), he was uttering words that would prove timeless. I said in the last chapter that Jesus was urging us to look within ourselves for the answers we seek. But he was also saying something else, something full of challenge, interest and purpose. Jesus was suggesting that in our earthly kingdom we have become separated from the true purposes of goodness, love and kindness – the kingdom of heaven – which describe the ultimate will of God. Greed and mediocrity have so made their way into our hearts and lives that courage and integrity sometimes appear to be lost. We only have to read the newspapers or glance at a television news bulletin to see how separated we have become from the goodness, love and kindness which should be abiding common values of our everyday living.

Far from being just another outdated religious term, 'the kingdom of heaven' as described by Jesus is a tremendously exciting, challenging and invigorating concept. It is something to be part of and something to work for. And it begins with you and me.

When you pray for guidance in your moments of serenity, you will feel yourself led to whatever part you may be called to play to contribute towards the building up of the kingdom of heaven within life as we know it. This 'kingdom thinking', as I would describe it, starts by finding fertile soil in your heart within which to grow. Then you can begin to feel less encumbered by whatever has previously been holding you back, and embark upon a radical review of your life and your outlook, so you can start to see just what it is that you are meant to do with the rest of your life.

Remember also not to get so mired in everyday worries and anxieties that you forget to look up and see the bigger picture. Jesus knew all about this, for on several occasions in his teachings he urged his listeners, 'Do not worry.'

On one of these occasions he said:

> I tell you, do not worry about your life, what you will eat or drink; or about your body, what you will wear. Is not life more important than food, and the body more important than clothes? ... Can any one of you by worrying add a single hour to your life? ... So do not worry, saying, 'What shall we eat?' or 'What shall we drink?' or 'What shall we wear?' ... But seek first his kingdom and his righteousness, and all these things will be given to you as well. (Matt. 6:25, 27, 31, 33)

All of us have worries, both large and small. All of us know from time to time the agony of not knowing how things will work out or what to do next. It is then that this search for the kingdom of heaven can help to centre us and allow us to separate the significant purposes from the insignificant, to concentrate upon the important instead of the trivial. As that wonderful timeless prayer of Dr Reinhold Niebuhr has it:

> Lord, give us grace to accept with serenity the things that cannot be changed, the courage to change the things which should be changed, and the wisdom to distinguish the one from the other.

Sometimes it is when things do go wrong that we find our true direction.

Anna was a former student of mine who failed to get her much longed-for place at Oxford University to study for an Arts degree. Distraught, she came to see me, uncertain about what to do next. At that time I had some contact with the Vietnamese boat refugees in Hong Kong and I suggested that she might like to spend some time out there working with the refugees. She agreed, and she went to Hong Kong for several months.

When she returned she got in touch to tell me that she had decided to go to university in London, to study medicine. She had been so moved by the experience of seeing such poverty and ill health in such cramped conditions that she felt compelled to do something to help. Anna had found her purpose; she qualified as a doctor and she is now a world-recognised expert in her field.

Anna's life path was changed when she had to face rejection and find a way to recover and move on. For others, their purpose may be clear from the start.

Another former pupil of mine, Alan, was passionate about his football team, Dundee. When he was sixteen and still at school, Alan researched, wrote and sold a regular fanzine for his team. One day he came to me and asked if he could be excused from a rugby match in order to go and sell his magazine! His enthusiasm and commitment shone from him, so I agreed to let him have the extra time. Today Alan Pattullo is a highly regarded senior sports correspondent for the *Scotsman* newspaper.

One of my great mentors was George Thomas, Lord Tonypandy, former Speaker of the House of Commons – the first person in history to hold that celebrated office at the invitation of two different governments. George, as he was more commonly known throughout Wales, and even beyond, was an extraordinary man: modest, wise and gracious.

He always said that he owed much to his mother and to her deep and lasting wisdom, which he drew upon every day of his life. After his father abandoned the family, George's mother brought him and his siblings up alone. In his autobiography, *Mr Speaker*, George remembers how she remained cheerful at all times, rising above their impoverished circumstances. One of his fondest memories was of her washing the dishes after meals and singing 'Count your many blessings, and name them one by one' as she worked. George gradually began to realise, through his early life, that his mother was working, despite all her difficulties, to bring about 'the kingdom of heaven' on her part of this earth. Small wonder, then, that in later life he would, in his marvellous mellifluous voice, proclaim, 'The man isn't born yet who does not need an anchor in his life. No man reaches his or her full stature until they have a realisation of deep and abiding spiritual values for life.'

The anchor of George Thomas's life was the living example of Jesus of Nazareth. Having seen such broken-heartedness and dispiritedness in his early life in the valleys of Wales, George 'stepped out of the drawer' and set out to make the world a better, braver and fairer place. And despite his tough start in life, he became a schoolteacher and then, later, a Member of Parliament, representing his beloved Tonypandy.

A deeply spiritual man, George recognised the abiding common sense of Jesus of Nazareth when he told the parable of the men who built their respective houses on shifting sand and on solid rock. For George, as had been the case for his mother, no matter what the world threw at him in terms of circumstances and the needs of others, his 'rock' was the ever-present awareness that 'the kingdom of heaven on earth' was well worth working for. That was the purpose of his soul.

Let the lights come on

So what might be your steps on the road to discovering or rediscovering your purpose?

First of all, realise that no experience, however tough or regrettable at the time, is wasted. We are each like a piece of marble in the hands of the great Sculptor, who sees and discerns our inner shape and beauty even before we are born.

If we can 'let go and let God', then we will be committing our lives into God's hands. In the calmness of being still and of knowing God, our hearts become serene – and in that serenity and inner calmness we allow God to speak to us. Perhaps he is calling us to fundamental changes in outlook, in the company we keep, or in the concepts that we appear to value.

When Cliff Morgan, former international rugby player turned BBC broadcaster, was interviewing the actress Liv Ullman, he asked her, 'Liv, when was it you realised you could become a great actress?'

There was a rather long radio pause and then she answered, 'Do you know, Cliff, I think it was when I was surrounded by my family and friends, those to whom I could go at any time knowing that they would neither laugh at my dreams nor mock at my failures. It was then that I realised I could become good.'

There was another short silence before she added, 'It was almost as if the lights came on.'

That too can be your experience, however uncertain you feel, however held back by a previous comment or incident or 'failure'. There are those who know you and love you and want the best for you and want you to realise the purpose of your soul.

More than that, and deep within your heart, the great Listener and Sculptor merely awaits your first intake of breath that will let you openly, honestly and unreservedly say, 'Please help me make sense of all this. You have shown me who I am, now please guide me to where and what you want me to be.'

Let the lights inside you come on.

Four questions to ask yourself

A while ago I was invited to speak at a rather theoretical conference in London on the theme of leadership.

Recognising he had an audience that would debate things to death and still miss the point, one of the speakers recognised a different approach was needed. So rather briliantly, he simply said, 'I have four questions for you:

What do you stand for?

What do you hope for?

How would you like to be remembered?

What would you do with your life if you had no chance of failing?'

The audience were then asked to share the answers with those on either side of them. The whole place buzzed with interest and excitement – the change of tack had been extremely effective!

Afterwards I thought long and hard about those questions and how effectively they can be used to bring us closer to discovering our true purpose. So, with kind permission from my friend at the conference, I put them to you now.

WHAT DO YOU STAND FOR?

It was author Mark Twain who said, 'A true friend is someone who knows all about you and still likes you.' How well do your friends and family know you? If children or family or friends were to describe you in your absence, what would they say about you? Would they speak of your core beliefs, your fundamental principles and the values by which and through which

45

you try to live your life? Perhaps they might not be too sure, in which case it might be wise to reflect on why this is the case. Are you too cautious about defining yourself and the things you believe in?

What are the limits and boundaries to which you adhere? In other words, what are your 'non-negotiables'? Sometimes in this world of diversity and complexity it is difficult to know what to stand for and when, particularly given the creeping influence of political correctness – much of which is helpful and right, yet which by imposing strict rules can seem so unnecessary and debilitating to the impulses of human kindness.

During my time as an army chaplain with the Parachute Regiment and later The Black Watch, a formidably impressive Sunday school teacher once said to me, at a time of difficult decision-making when petty differences and arguments were clouding the important issues, 'Padre, up with this I will not put!'

It is important to know what pushes us too far and what we will not put up with. When we know what we stand for, we can begin to build towards what we hope for.

WHAT DO YOU HOPE FOR?

What is it that you most hope for? For many of us it is to do with the happiness and well-being of our family. There is an old Texan saying, 'You can only be as happy as your least happy child', which I think is very true. If you have a child who is in distress or troubled in some way, then this will be more significant than pretty well everything else in your life and will form the basis of your hopes. But if everyone seems content, we can forget that these things matter to us so deeply. Do not let that happen.

Others may hope for a cleaner, safer, more environmentally sound world; or for the world to be a better, more responsible, more thoughtful, more loving and kinder place.

HOW WOULD YOU LIKE TO BE REMEMBERED?
If you know what you stand for, and what you hope for, now you can think about how you would most like to be remembered. Many a conference or a workshop in professional and business working life has been stopped in its tracks when such a question has been asked.

- 'Write down in a few sentences how you would like to be remembered.'
- 'Think ahead to your funeral. What will they say about you?'
- 'In your own mind take a trip forward in time and visit your own gravestone. What will be written there?'

These questions task us to find a succinct way to sum up what has been most important in our lives. In a similar vein, when you look back, what is it that you regret, or wish you had done differently? People often say that no one looks back and says, 'I wish I'd spent more time at the office,' and this is clearly true. But what is it that you wish you *had* been doing? Spending time with your family? Being creative? Studying? Getting involved with something worthwhile or some particular group of people?

WHAT WOULD YOU DO WITH YOUR LIFE IF
YOU HAD NO CHANCE OF FAILING?
We can so easily be held back by words and sayings from our past. Hurtful things tend to stick in our minds, so that, as if at the flick of a switch, we can hear that critical teacher, a thoughtless friend or clever enemy wound us to the core again with a phrase or a comment, reducing us to panic or paralysis. And in the wake of this it can become all too easy to retreat and to justify our lack of action by saying, 'Why me? Others are far better and more qualified. Why give people the chance to laugh at my dreams and mock my failures?'

Thinking about what you would do if there was no chance of failure or criticism can be eye-opening, because it can show you just how much you are letting things hold you back. With no chance of failure, we could soar to great heights, achieving wonderful successes.

What are you avoiding because you are afraid to fail? Now is the time to be brave, be proud of yourself and, in the words of Susan Jeffers, 'feel the fear – and do it anyway'.

Nelson Mandela borrowed the wonderful words of the American author and spiritual leader Marianne Williamson when, in his inauguration speech in 1994, he said:

> Our deepest fear is not that we are inadequate. Our deepest fear is that we are powerful beyond measure. It is our light, not our darkness, that most frightens us. We ask ourselves, who am I to be brilliant, gorgeous, talented, and fabulous? Actually, who are you not to be? You are a child of God. Your playing small doesn't serve the world. There's nothing enlightened about shrinking so that other people won't feel insecure around you. We are all meant to shine, as children do. We are born to make manifest the glory of God that is within us. It's not just in some of us, it's in everyone. And as we let our own light shine, we unconsciously give other people permission to do the same. As we are liberated from our own fear, our presence automatically liberates others.

In later years he often paraphrased those words to say:

> Who are you to be exceptional? Actually, who are you NOT to be exceptional?

The answers to the four questions asked above will give you a great deal of information that will help to make clear the purpose that is in your soul. Each and every one of us has a

God-given purpose, should we choose to grasp it, and it is in our exceptionality, as different and diverse human beings yet all loved by God, that we can indeed find the true purpose of our souls and so of our lives.

When what you stand for, what you hope for, the way you would like to be remembered and what you would do if you could not fail come together in seeking first the kingdom of heaven, wholeheartedly and unashamedly, then you will find courage, wisdom and purpose energising your mind and flowing through your heart. At that moment it is as if your heart and your head connect in such a way that you mentally know, emotionally feel and spiritually recognise the ultimate purpose of your soul.

When I was a student at Cambridge University, at the end of each evening service the Fitzwilliam College chaplain, Martin Baddeley, always gave us a final blessing, 'And now, let go and let God.' It was simple and yet powerful, and I never forgot it. It seemed to me like a reminder that each of our lives was a gift which we could choose to live purposefully in the service of others.

That choice was not so very different from the experience of the earliest disciples who, having heard about this rather remarkable and unusual man from Nazareth, one day found him watching them as they drew in their nets at the end of a long day's fishing. 'Come, follow me . . . and I will make you fishers of men' (Matt. 4:19 NIV). They left their nets, and their lives were never the same again.

There comes a moment, an inner crossroads of our lives, when all we can do in the hard-won serenity of our hearts is quietly and prayerfully to 'let go and let God'.

Never give up

The great car manufacturer Henry Ford once said:

You can do anything if you have enthusiasm. Enthusiasm is the yeast that makes your hopes rise to the stars. Enthusiasm is the sparkle in your eyes, the swing in your gait, the grip of your hand, the irresistible surge of will and energy to execute your ideas. Enthusiasts are fighters. They have fortitude. They have staying qualities. Enthusiasm is at the bottom of all progress. With it, there is accomplishment. Without it, there are only alibis.

The celebrated writer Ralph Waldo Emerson went even further, declaring, 'Nothing great was ever achieved without enthusiasm.'

To find your true purpose and carry it through, you will need enthusiasm. There will, without doubt, be times when you slow down, feel dispirited or want to give up. When that happens, remember what Abraham Lincoln said: 'I walk slowly, but I never walk backwards.' He was right. Pursuing the purpose of our lives may at times weigh us down and slow us up, but it will always carry us forward if we maintain our enthusiasm. And when fairness, kindness and faithfulness are matched with enthusiasm, there is a new spring in our step and an inner dynamism which rescues us from worries and regrets and which enables us to look courageously forward.

Comedian Michael McIntyre is a master of enthusiasm. Who can resist smiling when he skips onto the stage, beaming broadly and bouncing with cheeriness and energy? He is Britain's most successful comedian, with his own television series and the ability to fill London's vast O2 Arena five times over during his recent tour. Yet only a short time ago, Michael felt totally dispirited. After years of scratching out an existence on the fringes of the comedy circuit, he thought of giving up.

He tells the story of how he sat in a café in Edinburgh with his wife, after yet another year of going unnoticed at the famous summer festival, and wept. He was lucky to be booked as the reserve comedian at mediocre London clubs, only able to go on if one of the other performers didn't show up, and he didn't know how he would ever break through. But he made the decision to keep trying and, as word spread about his wonderful observational humour, he went from success to success.

When Michael McIntyre talks about his comedy, he says, 'I always thought "act" was a strange word – because this isn't my act, this is me.' And that sums up perfectly what it is to find your purpose. It is not something you choose to do; it is the essence of you.

Eric Liddell, the great Olympic runner, puts it wonderfully well in the film *Chariots of Fire* when he says:

> You came to see a race today. To see someone win. It happened to be me. But I want you to do more than just watch a race. I want you to take part in it. I want to compare faith to running in a race. It's hard. It requires concentration of will, energy of soul. You experience elation when the winner breaks the tape – especially if you've got a bet on it. But how long does that last? You go home. Maybe your dinner is burnt. Maybe you haven't got a job. So who am I to say, 'Believe, have faith' in the face of life's realities? I would like to give you something more permanent, but I can only point the way. I have no formula for winning the race. Everyone runs in her own way, or his own way. And where does the power come from, to see the race to its end? From within. Jesus said, 'Behold, the Kingdom of God is within you. If with all your hearts, you truly seek me, you shall ever surely find me.' If you commit yourself to the love of Christ, then that is how you run a straight race.[2]

We are all, in our own ways, running the race. Each one of us has a choice: either to live life purely for ourselves in the pursuit of selfish material gain, or to live our lives for the common good, for our families, for our community, for our country, for the building of the kingdom of heaven on earth.

John F. Kennedy, in his inauguration speech as President of the United States, put it this way: 'Think not of what your country can do for you, but of what you can do for your country.'

Another of my former mentors, a wonderful man, the Very Reverend Dr Ronald Selby-Wright, one of the best-known Church of Scotland ministers of his generation, put it in the form of a beautiful poem:

Do not pray for easy lives
Pray to be stronger men and women
Do not pray for tasks equal to your powers
Pray for powers equal to your tasks
Then the doing of your work and the living of your life shall
   be no miracle
But you shall be a miracle
Every day you will wonder at the richness of life
Which has come to you through the Grace of God.

Reflections

True purpose is rooted in the soul. Spend quiet time reflecting on what your purpose is and then 'let go and let God'. Trust that, with quiet determination, you will find what you are meant to be doing and be prepared for whatever is asked of you.

Jesus said, 'My command is this: Love each other as I have loved you' (John 15:12). When we take these words into our hearts and allow them gently and quietly to distil, we become infused and enthused with a deep quality of purpose. Our hearts are renewed, our souls are revived, because now we know that with integrity and authenticity we can live in the presence of Jesus of Nazareth and so according to his purposes for our lives.

Remember to practise 'kingdom thinking' and allow goodness and faith to grow in your heart, as you work to make this world a better, safer and more loving place.

Service

I don't know what your destiny will be, but one thing I do know: the only ones among you who will be really happy are those who have sought and found how to serve.

(Dr Albert Schweitzer)

Service is the wisdom which brings together the noblest aspects of serenity and purpose. With the serenity to go calmly and know ourselves, and a sure sense of our purpose in this world, we can put selfish wishes aside and find ways to offer others our love and support. And in doing so we are blessed, for there is no greater source of joy, fulfilment and meaning in life than through service to others. It is as if, in being of service to others, something previously dormant within our souls is given the oxygen it needs to spring to life.

Time after time, those who feel empty inside and see their lives as ultimately futile, often despite living in wealth and comfort, have found meaning and joy through service to others. There is no greater remedy for the blues, for self-pity, for self-obsession or for lack of direction in life, than to work for the good of others. There is a quality of inner contentment that is tangible and powerful that we often see in those for whom service is part of their being.

The American educational psychologist Joseph Campbell said, 'When we quit thinking primarily about ourselves and our self-preservation, we undergo a truly heroic transformation of consciousness.' This is a beautiful way of summing up what happens when we give to others, especially when what we are giving is our own time, energy and effort.

We live in an age when there is a great deal of mindless activity available – sitting at a computer surfing the Net, or in front of the television watching 'reality' shows may be fun for a while, but ultimately there is very little satisfaction in it. There is not much satisfaction for those who take part in the 'reality' shows either; many end up disillusioned and feeling they are losers, and even the winners sometimes wish they had not taken part.

In 1999 Bart Spring in't Veld won the very first series of *Big Brother* on Dutch television. Celebrity status followed for him and for Sabine, the woman with whom he had sex on television with 15 million Dutch viewers looking on. Their 'relationship' lasted a month. Three days after emerging from the house, Bart had his first breakdown. He spent the next two years in what he called 'oblivion'. He made 'an insane amount of money', but burned his way through most of it.

'I was a false saint,' he says. 'I felt that the whole country had gone mad. I found the whole country dumbed down . . . I had contempt for a society for which fame is an end in itself.' He became reclusive and suffered more breakdowns, seeking refuge in drinking, womanising and the soft drugs he called 'my rescue from insanity'. In his continuing pain and disappointment, Bart called out to others: 'Get a life, read a book, do some community service.'

What is so encouraging is that many, many people, across the world, are responsive to just that call. One of the most heartening aspects of the economic downturn has been that people are re-evaluating their lives, discovering that material things are not really so important, choosing to give some of their time to helping others. Even though a lot of people are worse off financially than they were a year or two ago, they are giving more.

Those who have begun giving have discovered the wonderful sense of fulfilment to be gained from hard work in the service of those who need help. And this is happening at all levels of society. Even celebrities are doing their bit, joining in schemes to help developing countries not just by giving money but by putting on a hard hat and helping to build a school or a hospital where it is desperately needed. Many are discovering that, while it is commendable to give money, there is far more to a real sense of giving than simply handing over some cash.

No matter how much or how little you have, no matter how full or empty your life, it is always worth making time for service to others. There is no substitute for this kind of giving, and nothing more important to the well-being of our souls.

At Columba 1400, the Community and International Leadership Centre which we run on the Isle of Skye in Scotland, we teach this. The most important component of our leadership courses is service, and this is equally true for those youngsters who come along from the tough realities of a Glasgow or London housing estate as it is for those who come from the upper management teams of successful businesses.

Young people from tough realities come each week to Columba 1400. Each day they discuss and centre on one of our core values: Awareness, Focus, Creativity, Integrity and Perseverance. But it is the final core value, Service, that brings the whole experience together. Having considered where they have come from, how they have become the product of their upbringing and environment, these brave young people decide to be themselves, to be the people they were created to be. And more often than not this happens when, to borrow the words of that first 'successful' Dutch *Big Brother* contestant, they get a life and commit to some service.

It is so often through service to others that they realise they are not simply 'a waste of space', that they are not only loving but also loved and lovable, and 'the light comes on'. That glorious self-discovery of meeting one's real self for the first time enables a previously damaged, troubled young soul to find out who he or she really is.

I believe that, to paraphrase an ancient prayer, 'In true service is perfect freedom.' I believe we serve God best by serving others. Frère Roger of the Taizé Community described it this way:

> All who choose to love and say it with their life are led to ask themselves one of the most compelling questions of all: how can we ease the pain and the torment of others, whether they are close at hand or far away?'[1]

Perhaps you are already on that journey, or perhaps you need to return to base, to reconfigure your compass in a new direction. If you do, then it can seem daunting. Where to begin? If you are hesitating, then remember the words of that great Scottish mountaineering pioneer W. H. Murray, 'It all begins with the first step.' You do not have to find all the answers at once, just start with a step in the direction in which you intend to go. Remember that others have been this way before, so you are never alone. And remember Jesus of Nazareth, who showed us what it truly means to give.

The inspiration of Jesus

So often when we take the decision to be of service, we are inspired by example. This may be the example of someone whom we have known and loved, who lived in such a beautiful and generous way that we would want to be like them. To have known such a person is enriching and encouraging. But the most inspiring example of all is Jesus of Nazareth. He lived his life in the service of others, putting their needs above his own, and never failing those who needed his help, sustenance and faith. His was the original call to service, and in answering that call and making a difference to the lives of others, we will make a difference in our own lives too.

The perfect example of Jesus of Nazareth encourages us to be sincere in our love and to practise hospitality and service wherever and whenever we can. He was enormously courageous, prepared to be out there, among all the hostilities he faced from the Jews who disapproved of him, and the Romans who simply disapproved of Jews, and yet to live a life so representative of goodness and of unconditional love. And it was because of this that so many men and women were drawn irresistibly to him.

His goodness and unconditional love were so authentic and transparent that they shone out, in contrast to the idle mediocrities of those whose outdated practices enabled them to place fear in the hearts of others. In those days the self-righteous few were able to 'lord it' in unimaginable ways over the dispossessed many.

The world into which Jesus of Nazareth came over two thousand years ago was as fragmented and directionless as our world is today. Men and women then were as deeply dissatisfied as many are today. Society was every bit as broken and yet over-regulated, certainly by the religious authorities – to the extent that ordinary men and women and families were looking for someone or something to mend the broken pieces.

Jesus arrived into a world of such complex religiosity that celestial observance had become more important than earthly behaviour, and his teaching and his attitude to life were so very different from those of the religious authorities of his day that they created shockwaves. It is hard for us now to imagine the extraordinary effect of Jesus' teachings in the Sermon on the Mount. Here is a veritable manifesto of how men and women should aspire to treat one another and to address the ongoing issues of each and every day. There are lessons and insights on poverty, sadness, humility, kindness and purity, peace and persecution. Tricky topics such as murder, adultery, divorce, revenge, philanthropy, fasting and prayer come to life in clearly recognisable, practical and readily applicable thinking. Jesus encourages his listeners, then and now, to resist the attractions of materialism and to build up 'treasure in heaven'. In that way there will be no need to worry as much as we do, nor to judge others. In our prayers we are to 'ask, seek, knock', for then we shall find that the foundations of our lives will be built on rock and not on shifting sands.

No wonder, then, that Jesus' early ministry should have been greeted with such astonishment and acclaim. Here was an ordinary man who spoke with remarkable authority. His words were those of kindness and understanding and yet without even a hint of personal gain or self-aggrandisement.

Jesus' approach enabled individual men, women and children to feel that he was talking very personally, almost one on one, to each of them. He spoke of healing and mending, of contrition and forgiveness, of renewal and inspiration.

Most inspiring of all, he practised what he preached. Imagine the surprise of the earliest disciples when at the Last Supper Jesus insisted on washing their feet – the humblest and yet most reassuring act of physical care and attention, as today countless physiotherapists and reflexologists, and their patients, would readily testify.

In this, and in so many other ways, Jesus lived up to the best and most authentic of biblical teaching. As he said, 'So in everything, do to others what you would have them do to you, for this sums up the Law and the Prophets' (Matt. 7:12).

Here was a leader with whose words and actions ordinary people could identify. His manifesto was exacting, but he also had enormous compassion: 'Come to me, all you who are weary and burdened, and I will give you rest' (Matt. 11:28).

Jesus was speaking to the inner hearts and minds of those who would come to listen to him, as indeed he does to this day.

The love that Jesus gave to all those around him transformed their discontent into wonder, inspiration and belief in the power of love. And so it has been for those of us who have come since. The love Jesus gave enables all of us to feel loved and therefore lovable and this in turn leads us to an irresistible inner desire to be of use and service to others.

In 2 Corinthians 5 we read, 'For Christ's love compels us . . . he died for all, that those who live should no longer live for themselves' (vv. 14–15).

Often inspiration can be found in one line, one story or one memorable parable in his life, which leads us to review our own lives and to choose the path we want to follow. Certainly this was true for me. Everything which I have attempted to do in my life, not least in endeavouring to be there for others in the difficulties and challenges of daily living, can be traced back to the resonant and powerful truth of a simple story of love and care told by perhaps the greatest storyteller of all time. I have told the story in the previous chapter of my wonder and excitement, as a small boy in Sunday school, when I heard the parable of the Good Samaritan. In finding this the inspiration for the way I wanted to lead my life, I know I am by no means alone, for many over the centuries have found in this parable, or another of the stories and parables told by Jesus, that which shaped the future conduct and path of their lives. A far cry from the doctrinarian insistence of the Sadducees and the Pharisees on believing everything according to the 'letter of the law'. What forces for good have been released in simply listening and responding to the words of Jesus of Nazareth, over successive generations?

Perhaps this is what the famous nineteenth-century professor of science and religion Henry Drummond had in mind when he wrote, 'We hear much of love to God; Christ spoke much of love to man. We make a great deal of peace with heaven; Christ made much of peace on earth.'

What is service?

There is a well-worn colloquialism which says, 'There's no point in being so heavenly minded that you are no earthly use!' But what does it mean to be of earthly use, or service, to others?

I think the simplest way to sum up the true nature of service is 'love in action'. When you act towards others with love, then you are able to be of service. Look for what you are able to do to ease the burdens and suffering of others, whether they are close to you or strangers. When you show someone else that they are not alone in their hardships, then you are of service. When you ease the load of another, by sharing it, you are of service.

You can be of service every day, by speaking with kindness and being generous, thoughtful and encouraging towards those around you.

And you can be of service, specifically, by getting involved with something that needs doing. Choose always to help those whose need is genuine and who are unable to help themselves. Look for those areas in which you will be of most use. Perhaps you will want to get involved in a project which benefits your community, or to work with the elderly, the sick or the infirm. Perhaps you will be able to give regular time each week to make a contribution, or set aside a week occasionally, or just help on an ad hoc basis.

There are all kinds of ways of serving others, not all of them obvious. Look for something to get involved with that is of real interest to you and will be enjoyable – being of service is not necessarily about being 'noble' in doing something you do not want to do; it can be fun, and a source of interest and knowledge. Do it with a willing and open heart, giving of your-self and your knowledge and experience.

Tom decided he wanted to do something for his local community and, after looking around at some of the projects in need of support, he chose to become a tour guide for Highgate Cemetery, in north London. This extraordinary cemetery is the resting place of many of the greatest Victorians of their era, and every year hundreds of people come from all over the world, not only to visit the grave of the great Socialist thinker, historian and revolutionary Karl Marx, but also of writers such as George Eliot and artists such as Christina Rossetti and Henry Moore. It is a place of great peace and beauty, filled with intricately carved statues and memorials, and it is run entirely by volunteers, who not only give up their time, but who study the history of the cemetery and those who lie there, in order to be able to give informed tours to the visitors. For several years Tom spent every other Saturday as a volunteer, and he credited this regular involvement and commitment with helping him to recover from the frequent bouts of depression which had previously blighted his life.

Annie, a shy woman who lived alone, decided she wanted to be involved with nature, so she volunteered for a conservation group in the New Forest, where she lived. They met regularly to work together on projects vital to the preservation of this beautiful National Park, clearing ponds, safeguarding plants and caring for the habitats of the wild animals there. Working for several hours at a time, along-side a group of other people, Annie found the hard, physical effort both exhausting and exhilarating. She made friends with other volunteers and gradually became more confident and outgoing as a result and eventually Annie decided, after many years on her own, to share a flat with one of her new friends.

Sue was a busy mum with three children and a part-time job, but she still found time to volunteer a few hours a week for her local hospice, sitting with the patients, chatting to them and helping to look after them. 'Don't you find it hard being around people who are dying?' a friend asked her. 'No,' Sue said, 'I find it wonderful. Every time I'm there I see courage, humour, acceptance, joy and friendship in the patients, the staff and the visitors. It's a place of peace and wisdom, and I'm so glad I can be a part of it.'

These volunteers, and many thousands like them, work for others, as part of their everyday lives. And all of them feel enriched, wiser and happier for the experience. Service is a gift you give to others, but the gift you receive through it is far greater.

Psychologist Dr Robert Holden, who founded the hugely successful 'Happiness Project' which runs courses training people in how to be happy, says, 'There is a strong connection between happiness and the wellbeing of others. When we're anxious, depressed and neurotic we tend to become completely concerned with ourselves and go within. Yet we can counteract inner emptiness by getting involved and giving and when we switch our attention from having to giving we become happier.'

Are you ready to make a difference?

Every one of us can make a difference to the lives of others.

Some people choose what they wish to do; others feel the task chooses them. It can happen when you see something that needs doing and think, 'Why is no one doing something about this? Surely if a few of us got together we could make a difference.'

Some of the great social reformers of the past have attested to such feelings – a sense of knowing that something must change, yet not being quite sure what is required to begin.

William Wilberforce was a young politician who had yet to make his mark when he received a letter from John Newton, the former slave trader and later Anglican priest in the City of London and celebrated author of many hymns, including 'Amazing Grace'. Newton wrote:

> I believe you are the Lord's servant, and are in the post which He has assigned you; and though it appears to me more ardu-ous, and requiring more self-denial than my own, I know that He who has called you to it can afford you strength according to your day.

Such encouragement from a respected person who, from the slave trade to the ministry, had literally been to hell and back, inspired the young William to set out on his life's purpose. After he received this letter, in the autumn of 1786, he wrote in his diary, 'What madness I said to myself, is this! Here have I been throwing away my time all my life passed!'

He did not throw away another moment. For the rest of his life he worked to free those bound in slavery, and decades later his struggle brought about the formal abolition of the slave trade.

Throughout history there have been countless moments, some very well recorded and others less so, when a connection, a conversion, has happened in the life of an individual when he or she is able to say, 'That's for me. I am ready to commit. I am ready to serve.'

Giovanni Francesco di Bernadone was the son of an Italian nobleman who lived a spoiled and idle life of merrymaking and enjoyment. But Giovanni had misgivings about his wealthy lifestyle, and one day he felt compelled to dismount from his horse and rush to embrace a man who was suffering from leprosy. So began the life of service of St Francis of Assisi who, against all sorts of opposition, parental, personal and governmental, pursued the life that he felt he was meant to follow and founded the order of Franciscan monks who to this day live in complete poverty, serving others.

It was St Francis who wrote, 'It is by forgetting self that one finds self,' and in this there is a great truth. When you are able to forget about yourself and stop focusing on your own needs and wants, eventually you will find your true self, the inner self that connects with the divine.

Those moments of realisation, such as that of St Francis, are profound, but that does not mean they are straightforward. Doubts, fears and uncertainties are part of the journey for those who decide to give their lives in service.

Such were the feelings of a young Indian woman from a very wealthy and high-caste background who began to realise the emptiness of so much of her life. She made her way into the slums of Calcutta to find the Sisters of Charity, led by Mother Teresa, and asked if she could be of any help.

Mother Teresa and the Sisters welcomed her warmly and then suggested that she might like to spend several days out in the streets of Calcutta working with them. She gladly accepted, but it was not long before this privileged young woman was really struggling. Horrified by the squalor and disease she encountered, she became uncertain about whether she could carry on, so much so that she asked to speak to Mother Teresa herself. Something must have happened in that conversation, because the young woman returned the next day to her work on the streets where, without hesitation or complaint, she tended the sores of those who could not walk, cleared out maggots from the wounds of those who could not heal and cleaned the bodies of those who could not reach or find water to wash.

When Mother Teresa asked later how she was getting on, she replied, 'Mother, you were right. I simply could not have done any of that in my own strength or power. It was the love of Christ within me that enabled me to do it and now I am ready to serve.'

This young woman had discovered for herself, from the inside out, the inexpressible joy of what it means to 'be there' unreservedly, uncomplainingly and unconditionally in the service of others.

In her book *In My Own Words*, Mother Teresa wrote:

There are some people who, in order not to pray, use as an excuse the fact that life is so hectic that it prevents them from praying. This cannot be. Prayer does not demand that we interrupt our work, but that we continue working as if it were a prayer. It is not necessary to always be meditating, nor to consciously experience the sensation that we are talking to God, no matter how nice this would be. What matters is being with Him, in His will. To love with a pure heart, to love everybody, especially to love the poor, is a 24-hour prayer.

And whether someone has very great faith or little faith or none, there can be an inner voice which says, 'This way of giving, in the service of others, is there for you.' When that moment comes, do we grasp it firmly with both hands, or do we let it pass? Each one of us has the choice; every time we see somewhere we could make a difference, we have that choice.

Ken Carter, a successful businessman and former high school basketball champion, was asked again and again if he would coach his old high school team. Time and time again he refused, until, watching the team in one match, he saw their potential and the difference that his coaching might make to their lives both on and off the basketball court. He changed his mind and said he would give it his best.

The difficulties which Ken encountered were beautifully depicted in the film *Coach Carter*. Through all the trials and obstacles – and there were many – Ken held himself and his team to sound core values and principles, which included respecting one another and themselves. As their discipline and self-respect increased, the team began to believe in themselves and in each other, and they went on to achieve remarkable success.

Not only did Coach Ken Carter produce a champion basketball team on court, he also produced several champions in life. Young men who previously would almost certainly have been condemned to a life of abuse, addiction and despair found their own 'inner greatness' and went on to lead happy and successful lives. Amazing as it may seem, I believe each one of us has it within us to be a Coach Carter – or at least a member of his team!

One of the nicest and most heart-warming examples of the effects of service can be found in British television's recent *Secret Millionaire* series. Each week someone who has made millions through their own hard work goes out to a poor community somewhere in Britain, often the one the millionaire came from, and goes undercover for a week or so. During this time, posing as a voluntary worker, the millionaire gets involved with local projects. At the end of this incognito time, the millionaire chooses which people or projects he or she feels deserve some extra help and donates some money. But the power of the programme is not in seeing who gets the money, but in seeing the effect on the millionaire of getting involved with those in need. Week after week we see someone who previously has thought about little other than the hard work of running a business, transformed by the act of giving – not money, but time and involvement. Often the millionaire chooses to stay involved with the projects which have touched his or her heart. In helping others less fortunate, these millionaires enrich their own lives.

What many of the millionaires discover for the first time is the true joy of giving. The money they have made takes on new meaning when they are able to use it to help those who need it. And their own involvement means that they begin to re-evaluate their lives.

One of the millionaires was Liz Jackson from Basingstoke, who runs a telemarketing business. Married, with a small daughter, she started the company at the age of twenty-five and turned it into a huge success, despite going blind at the age of twenty-six. Liz went to Lewisham in south London for the programme, and her experiences there changed her. She became involved with three charities and afterwards she said that being on the show had profoundly transformed her life. 'It reaffirmed my view of how inspirational it can be to serve others,' she said. 'I definitely feel happier since participating in the programme, as it taught me greater gratitude and that is surely the route to joy.'

Light a candle in the darkness

Sometimes the global challenges of economics, poverty, hunger, injustice, environment and climate can produce a seemingly endless list of despair and hopelessness and we can become overwhelmed by the magnitude of the problem that might lie ahead of us. It can seem too vast, too impossible. 'What on earth can I do to make a difference to such a huge problem?' you might ask.

Yet we should never become despondent, for so often it is the little things which ultimately count for the most. How good it is, at times like this, to remind ourselves that we can make a difference, 'you in your small corner and I in mine'.

And how much more powerful it is, then, to realise that when your light and mine are brought together with others across the barriers of belief or background or continent, we can provide a veritable torch of goodness, love and light, to encourage and inspire others in the darkness.

> Several times I have been with our family or a small group to visit the Taizé Community in the south of France. One of the most moving aspects of an Easter week pilgrimage is the Good Friday evening service when the whole worship area – encompassing literally thousands of individuals and families from all the continents of the world – will be plunged into darkness, followed by a period of silence. A candle is then lit and that candle lights another, and so on and on until there are thousands of candles burning in the darkness, radiating a brightness and beauty that no electric light could ever emulate, and no poet or writer could adequately describe.

What we see happening in the gathered multinational community of Taizé is a living representation of how St Paul interpreted the life and example of Jesus of Nazareth to those early, persecuted followers in Rome:

> Do not conform to the pattern of this world, but be transformed by the renewing of your mind. Then you will be able to test and approve what God's will is – his good, pleasing and perfect will. (Rom. 12:2)

A Chinese proverb has it thus: 'It is better to light a candle than to curse the darkness.' But there are those who live in darkness because they are fearful, or believe that lighting a candle

– taking that first step – is too difficult, too complicated or indeed simply impossible.

Ask yourself: are you ready for such a challenge? Are you ready to be there for and alongside others, and to light a candle in the darkness?

Go *the extra mile*

Sometimes it is hard for us to 'go the extra mile' or to 'give away one of our coats' as Jesus would encourage us to do. It is not easy to give away what is valuable to us, or to put in extra effort on someone else's behalf.

Most of us are so busy with the treadmill of our lives – work, partners, parents, children and the many demands we feel upon us. We feel we are managing pretty well, things are just about sorted, but we have no time or space to think of giving service to others. It is a great thing to do, we think, but I shall have to put it to one side for now and get back to it later.

Yet when we do go the extra mile, or when we are on the receiving end of somebody else's extra mile of kindness and service, then the depth and richness of our feelings can be unimaginable.

For many of us it may be a truly unexpected realisation that, despite the demands on our lives, we do indeed have the time, the capacity and the ability to become a 'second-miler' – those who will go the extra mile to help and support others.

A very loving and likeable father, whose son had been involved in a serious accident, came to see me. He said that while he had respect for the faith and practice of his parents in their family church life, for himself he had to acknowledge his own agnosticism, bordering on atheism. Yet he had been emotionally bowled over by the love, care and kindness which had been shown to him and his family in their hour of deepest need. These 'second-milers' had so touched his heart that something deeply spiritual was happening within his soul, a transformation he had not thought possible.

One of the most extraordinary and uplifting examples in recent years has been that of Nelson Mandela. Throughout his twenty-seven years in prison, his presidency and his life since, he has been a living example of what it means, as a 'second-miler', to discover that in true service is perfect freedom.

The South Africa correspondent of the *Independent*, John Carlin, wrote in 1994:

One of the many sad events that have accompanied the birth of democracy in South Africa was the death last month of John Harrison, BBC Television South African correspondent. An hour and a half after the news reached us in Johannesburg that John had been killed in a car crash, the phone rang at his home. A friend of John's wife Penny answered it.

'Hello. This is Nelson Mandela. Could I speak to Mrs Harrison please?'

The friend's first reaction was to assume this was a particularly tasteless crank call. But the man on the phone persevered and eventually persuaded her that he really was who he said he was. Penny went to the phone. It was a particularly frenetic time for Mandela, with the election campaign and the Bophuthatswana crisis raging at the time, not to mention the perennial Buthelezi question and the slaughter in Natal, but this was no perfunctory gesture, and certainly no vote-catching exercise. Mandela spoke to Penny for nearly half an hour. I have no idea how the conversation went, nor do I have any desire to pry. But I would imagine that he did the only thing one can do of any value in such circumstances. He would have conveyed his solidarity in suffering by reminding her that he too had lost a loved one in a car crash, one of his sons, while he was in prison on Robben Island.

A month later, during an ANC rally in Durban, Mandela spotted Mrs Harrison's friend among the journalists. He came up to her, said hello and asked, 'How's Penny doing?'[2]

What a wonderful example of love in action, making the time and taking the trouble to go the second mile. There are many such examples in the life of Nelson Mandela, a man who could be forgiven for bitterness, but who shows only love.

His example, and those of the many others who lead lives of service, give us footsteps in which to follow. Each time you do something for another human being, you fight back against the darkness. There can be no more worthwhile goal in life.

Reflections

Think of a time when someone has been there for you, offering you a listening ear, warmth or other support, and allow your heart to fill with gratitude for their generosity.

Spend time quietly reflecting on what service means to you, and the part it plays in your life. In what ways do you help others, those close to you and the wider community? Could you do more? Have you crossed the road or gone the extra mile to be there for others? Do they know of your desire to be there for them and to make a difference?

Remember that real lasting change does not necessarily happen in big initiatives, it happens one on one, one by one, and then in partnership. And it all begins with the first step. Here are the words spoken of Archbishop Oscar Romero:

This is what we are about: we plant seeds that one day will grow.

We water seeds already planted, knowing that they hold future promise. We lay foundations that will need further development. We provide yeast that produces effects beyond our capabilities. We cannot do everything and there is a sense of liberation in realising that. This enables us to do something, and do it very well. It may be incomplete, but it is a beginning, a step along the way, an opportunity for God's grace to enter and do the rest. We may never see the end results, but that is the difference between the master builder and the worker. We are workers, not master builders; ministers, not messiahs. We are prophets of a future not our own.[3]

The Three Principles

All it takes for evil to prosper is for good men
and women to say and do nothing.

(Edmund Burke)

If the three wisdoms are the fundamental building blocks to a life led with meaning, then the three principles offer the guidance we need as we choose our priorities and goals and travel life's path.

Just as the three wisdoms offer the foundations we need, giving us courage and commitment and keeping us grounded in the face of all that would blow us off course, so the three principles offer the tools with which we can build lives of value and purpose, led in the pursuit of what is good and worthwhile.

The first principle is *People before Process*. It teaches that we must never get so embroiled in the rules and red tape that we forget about people. Life today is full of checks and measures, procedures and forms to fill in. But what matters is the people around us, their feelings, needs and rights, and any organisation, large or small, needs to keep its heart as well as its head, and care for the people who are part of it.

The second principle is *Wisdom before Knowledge*. We live in a society where knowledge is considered to be of ultimate importance and those who can demonstrate it, via exam passes and qualifications, are lauded. Yet knowledge is not the same as wisdom, which takes itself far more lightly, yet has greater depth and insight, love and understanding. We all need to learn to trust our inner wisdom, and that of others, and to value and appreciate it, for it will lead us, with unerring certainty, in the right direction.

Finally there is the principle of *Integrity before Politics*. So often we know when something is not right or fair, but feel helpless to 'buck the system' and act on it. To have integrity means to be willing to put what is right, fair and just before what is expedient, dictated by the system or expected of us. When integrity comes first, we have the courage to stand up for ourselves and others and to fight for truth.

Together these three principles give us a tool-kit with which to handle whatever tough choices and decisions we face in life. When we put people, wisdom and integrity first, then we travel lightly, knowing that all will be well.

People Before Process

An organisation which concerns itself unduly with
procedures has lost faith in its ultimate aims.

(Hegel)

We live in an age when someone somewhere always seems to
be checking up on us, wanting to know more about our lives.
We are monitored, given rules to follow, advised and chided
by government, the media, multitudinous organisations and
committees.

Health and safety has taken on the mantle of Big Brother
and become the source of endless killjoy orders: Christmas
trees in public places are taken down in case they fall on someone, conker fights are banned in case a child gets hurt, council
employees are issued with a directive about how to hold onto a
banister properly, and parents have to be police-checked to help
out in their children's school.

Of course there are times when security is a genuine issue.
We understand why there are CCTV cameras in town centres,
and why we must be scrutinised and searched at airports. But
do we need to be watched every moment of the day, or told
what foods we should be eating, or have our children tested,
examined, regulated and categorised over and over again? We
have come to value targets so much that we have forgotten to
target values. And many of us have come to feel that people
take second place to process.

This is often true inside the workplace too. All too often,
bureaucracy chokes creativity. As meetings are called to discuss
other meetings and directives fly around like confetti, the

workforce often feel unappreciated, uncared for and, because of this, unmotivated. It is hard to give your all when you feel that those in charge do not recognise or care who you are or what you do.

We live in a time when many people work incredibly long hours, mostly because they feel they must in order to keep their jobs. But are those hours being productively, creatively used? Or are they simply being endured, in an atmosphere of fear or resentment?

Process has become so puffed up with self-importance that there is a whole new language associated with it. Terms like transparency, accountability, governance, project execution and performance goals are bandied about, while meaning very little to most people. And so often, when these terms are used in proliferation, what is missing is any spirit of integrity, authenticity and trustworthiness – not to mention a helping of common sense!

The principle of people before process is more of a challenge now than it has ever been, but it is vital, because it reminds us that we are, above all, human, and that we are all part of the human race together. What matters most, in every situation and every workplace, is people. And people are individuals, with a vast variety of ideas, beliefs and abilities. They do not fit neatly into categories, they can think for themselves, they love to be appreciated and valued, and it is a wise organisation, or committee, or government department, which recognises this.

However, these very government departments, committees and organisations are also made up of people. So in the end, it is up to each of us, as individuals, to have this as a guiding principle in our daily lives: *people before process*. With this principle foremost, we will treat everyone we encounter with respect and consideration, and we will never allow the processes – the rules, regulations and red tape – to come before the needs and rights of others.

At the time of Jesus

In Jesus' time there were many who put process before people. Foremost among them were the Pharisees. The name means 'the separate ones' in Hebrew and they were one of three sects, or schools, into which Jews were divided at that time. They were the bureaucrats of their day, without whose nod little could happen.

The Pharisees were also known as Chasidim, which means 'loyal to God', but over time they became devoted, and extremist about, very narrow parts of their religious Law, and adhering to and administering these aspects of the Law became more important than the justice and fairness which the Law was supposed to uphold. In other words, the Pharisees became obsessed with the process of the Law, and could no longer see beyond it. They forgot that the whole point of any just and justifiable law is to benefit people. Because of their absorption with Law for its own sake, the Pharisees were blind to the message of Jesus, when he was in their very midst. Instead of recognising that all he was doing was putting people first, they became bitter and deadly opponents of him and his message and did all they could to stop him.

Jesus had very little time or patience for the Pharisees, or for the Sadducees, another more elitist sect, who were at loggerheads with the Pharisees but equally attached to law over the needs or rights of people. Jesus often pointed out in strong terms just what these supposedly religious groups were doing. 'For I tell you that unless your righteousness surpasses that of the Pharisees and the teachers of the law, you will certainly not enter the kingdom of heaven,' he told those who came to listen to him (Matt. 5:20).

Matthew, in the New Testament, describes Jesus' attitude in this way:

'How is it you don't understand that I was not talking to you about bread? But be on your guard against the yeast of the Pharisees and Sadducees.' Then they understood that he was not telling them to guard against the yeast used in bread, but against the teaching of the Pharisees and Sadducees. (Matt. 16:11–12)

Just as yeast causes bread to rise, it was sometimes used as a symbol of sinful pride which made people haughty and 'puffed up', and Matthew is clarifying here that this was Jesus' meaning.

In the following passage, also from Matthew, Jesus made his feelings about these law-makers even clearer:

The teachers of the law and the Pharisees . . . do not practise what they preach. They tie up heavy, cumbersome loads, and put them on other people's shoulders, but they themselves are not willing to lift a finger to move them. Everything they do is done for people to see: They make their phylacteries wide and the tassels on their garments long; they love the place of honour at banquets and the most important seats in the synagogues, they love to be greeted with respect in the marketplaces and to have people call them 'Rabbi'. But you are not to be called 'Rabbi', for you have only one Master and you are all brothers. And do not call anyone on earth 'father', for you have one Father, and he is in heaven. (Matt. 23:2–9)

And again:

Woe to you, teachers of the law and Pharisees, you hypocrites! You shut the door of the kingdom of heaven in people's faces. You yourselves do not enter, nor will you let those enter who are trying to. (Matt. 23:13–14)

Jesus is calling the Pharisees hypocrites, for they loved to be looked up to and honoured by the people, but did not in turn honour God or behave in the way that God would wish. He is saying that self-righteousness is not righteousness, and that God's true people are to live according to *all* of God's Word, not just certain parts that are most convenient or most to one's own liking.

Through these passages, and many others too, Jesus made it clear that he had no time for those who put their own limited views before the needs and rights of actual people. God wanted all people to love one another, like brothers, Jesus said, and that came before any other law.

The words of Jesus to the process-driven bureaucrats of his day are among the most courageous and telling in recorded history. What strength and courage it must have taken to go against the religious and civil customs of the day. He knew he was endangering himself by arousing their anger, but he refused to bow down to them and continued to speak the truth.

When the Pharisees commented on the fact that Jesus did not observe their hand-washing rituals, his response was clear and to the point.

> Now then, you Pharisees clean the outside of the cup and dish, but inside you are full of greed and wickedness. You foolish people! Did not the one who made the outside make the inside also? But now as for what is inside you – be generous to the poor, and everything will be clean for you. (Luke 11:39–41)

Jesus even went on to question the process whereby so much time was spent on calculating their giving to God,

> You give God a tenth of your mint, rue and all other kinds of garden herbs, but you neglect justice and the love of God. You

should have practised the latter without leaving the former undone. (Luke 11:42)

In his brave attacks on the rigid conformities of his day, Jesus was seeking to bring out how the outer-facing world of process and doing things right had taken precedence over the inner-facing world of people and doing the right thing. And beyond that, he was providing encouragement to those who were at the mercy of the law-givers, and he spoke up for the powerless and unprotected.

No wonder one of the experts in the law answered Jesus by saying, 'Teacher, when you say these things, you insult us also.' Jesus replied, 'And you experts in the law, woe to you, because you load people down with burdens they can hardly carry, and you yourselves will not lift one finger to help them' (Luke 11:45–46).

By any definition these are strong words, and clearly spoken from the heart. Yet they may be not so very far from our own feelings when we find ourselves hemmed in, bewildered and frustrated by bureaucracy that threatens to choke good intentions and block all meaningful, worthwhile action; what we often lack is the courage to speak them out.

The primary reason why God chose to intervene in history through the presence and example of Jesus of Nazareth was that the old covenant between God and his people had been broken again and again, to such an extent that at this point the dictatorial top-down teachers of those days had pretty well got everything sewn up – or so they thought. In order to feel good about yourself, to be sure of your own rectitude and importance, the tried and tested way was to follow the Law. The Pharisees and Sadducees vied with each other to be more important, stricter, more rigorous and more knowledgeable, and so to be more respected. In fact the reigns of people like the Pharisees and Sadducees, as indeed in various fundamentalist movements since, simply serve to protect the few and terrorise the many.

When Jesus came along, society was in many ways a fearful place to be, for so strong were the different religious, political and military authorities and so rigorous the possible penalties that, as has happened in occupied nations throughout history, people did not feel they could trust each other or be sure of anything.

No wonder, then, that the simple teachings and memorable phrases of Jesus should have been so inwardly nourishing to people struggling to make sense of the heavy, detailed theological rulings of those who were held to be wise. Crowds of listeners and followers flocked to him in greater numbers even than those visiting the temple each day. No wonder the authorities were worried and sought to silence him (though there were also those, even among the law-makers, who listened).

On one occasion a teacher of the Law who had been impressed with the level of debate asked Jesus, 'Of all the commandments, which is the most important?' (Mark 12:28). Jesus replied that the most important commandment was to love God with all your heart, soul, mind and strength, and that the second was to love your neighbour as yourself, adding, 'There is no commandment greater than these' (v. 31).

The teacher of the Law, who was clearly alert to the revolution taking place in men's and women's hearts in the presence of Jesus of Nazareth, told him that he was right. Then he added that 'to love him with all your heart, with all your understanding and with all your strength, and to love your neighbour as yourself is more important than all burnt offerings and sacrifices' (v. 33).

This, for those days, was astonishing stuff! Jesus said to him, 'You are not far from the kingdom of God' (v. 34).

The credit crunch

The worldwide credit crunch, or recession, which had such a major impact through 2008 and 2009 in international and global economic affairs, was a prime example of what goes wrong when those in authority put process before people. The bankers who put their own bonuses first, and in so doing threatened the future and livelihoods of so many people, were no different from the Pharisees and Sadducees of Jesus' time.

> I remember visiting an elderly gentleman one evening in 2009 when another 'worst yet' announcement came on the television news. This ethical and respected retired businessman looked on stunned, his eyes moist with tears. As a Second World War veteran and a family business entrepreneur of some distinction, he simply could not believe what he was hearing. 'We used to trust the banks,' he said. 'Bankers were meant. to be cautious people who kept us right. How could they act in that way when they knew that spiralling debt was feathering their own pockets and could ultimately only lead to the loss of thousands of jobs, people's livelihoods, people's family lives, disruption and despair?'

How indeed? These bankers were shielded by the pervading 'Teflon' non-stick approach to blame, an irresponsible culture of self-seeking and buck-passing, against a backcloth of huge salaries and short-term bonuses.

In the world of business I sometimes wonder how much our lauded business schools have been responsible for putting process before people and selective individual material prosperity before the wealth of the nation. Thankfully it seems that individual professors of business are beginning to realise that, as with so many things in life, if you begin with people, the processes flow more smoothly and effectively than when they are imposed from on high with no regard to the effects on people.

> A celebrated Professor of Leadership Development from one of America's distinguished universities was speaking at a conference I attended when, in a memorable aside from his prepared lecture, he stepped to one side of the podium and said, 'It has taken me all these years to realise that organisations are like engines and engines need oil and the oil of an organisation is her people.' Then, smiling broadly, he added, 'Do you know, it has taken me all these years to realise that for most people the soft stuff is the hard stuff.'

This is something that every individual, within every organisation and community, needs to act upon. Look after the soft stuff, and the hard stuff will get along just fine. The credit crunch brought with it a powerful message of people before process, and if we are to recover, rebuild and do things differently in the future, then we must take in this message.

Process in education

There is no better example of how process has taken predominance over people than in the British education system.

> When he spoke at an International Educational Conference in the University of Edinburgh, the Dalai Lama was asked by a member of the audience, 'What do you think of our education system?'
> The Dalai Lama began chuckling, to such an extent that the whole audience began to laugh as well. After the laughter, he said, 'Recently I was visiting in India. They too have the British Victorian education system.' And he began to chuckle again.

The Dalai Lama's short measured answer, bookended by laughter, made a highly resonant and effective point. Perhaps, in our first-world democracies, we have been educated in such a didactic top-down way that we have almost unwittingly celebrated only that which we can measure, rather than stopping to consider and appreciate the essential needs and creativities of our children.

The Latin word *educare* means to 'lead out', or to 'bring out the best', or, as John Buchan was wont to say, to 'elicit the inner greatness'. Yet so much of what our children are taught is simply aimed at getting them through exams and satisfying inspection bodies and government dictates.

When Baroness Helena Kennedy, one of the world's leading criminologists, was invited to speak at the Annual General Meeting of the General Teaching Council, she gave an inspiring address. Nothing in her remarks could have been more inspirational than the answer which she gave to the final question of the evening. A senior head teacher, well respected throughout the profession, rose and asked, 'Lady Kennedy, if you were Minister of Education for a day, what is the one thing you would do?'

Like a greyhound sprung from its trap, Baroness Kennedy made her way to the lectern and replied, 'If I were Minister of Education for a day, the one thing I would do is to stop measuring everything. I would give teachers the opportunity to do what they are good at, to practise that for which they were trained – to influence and challenge and inspire other people's children.'

The response she received was so enthusiastic that it would have been worthy of an ovation at the opera in La Scala, Milan. Baroness Kennedy had clearly struck a deep chord among that large audience of dedicated professionals, so many of whom felt frustrated by the need to endlessly test, assess and examine their pupils.

It is a relief when someone has the courage to say what so many have been thinking and feeling. There is a certain powerlessness when left-brained measurement-oriented thinking takes over, and to say, 'This is nonsense!' gives us the chance to take back the power and open up choices.

The following letter, often attributed to Abraham Lincoln, that great American president, was sent by a father to the head-master of his son's new secondary school:

He will have to learn, I know, that all men are not just and are not true. But teach him if you can the wonder of books . . . also give him quiet time to ponder the eternal mystery of birds in the sky, bees in the sun and flowers on a green hillside.

In school, teach him it is far more honourable to fail than to cheat. . .

Teach him to have faith in his own ideas, even if everyone tells him he is wrong.

Teach him to be gentle with gentle people and tough with the tough.

Try to give my son the strength not to follow the crowd when everyone is getting on the bandwagon. . .

Teach him to listen to all men; but teach him also to filter all he hears on a screen of truth, and take only the good that comes through.

Teach him, if you can, how to laugh when he is sad . . . Teach him there is no shame in tears.

Teach him to scoff at cynics and to be beware of too much sweetness . . . Teach him to sell his brawn and brain to the highest bidders, but never to put a price on his heart and soul.

Teach him to close his ears to a howling mob . . . and stand and fight if he thinks he is right.

Treat him gently, but do not cuddle him, because only the test of fire makes fine steel. Let him have the courage to be impatient . . . Let him have the patience to be brave. Teach him always to have sublime faith in himself, because then he will have faith in humankind.

This is a big order, but see what you can do . . . He is such a fine little fellow my son!

What the writer wanted for his son was for him to be open to his dreams and his life's purpose, and not to be closed in by a rigid conformity to any particular system. How relevant those words are to our education system today. When we can put the good of children before mere exam results, we will be a truly enlightened society.

In my own experience of living and working with young people of all ages over several years as a headmaster, father and mentor, I have realised time and time again that what counts in the human experience is encouraging people to own their inner solutions and realisations for themselves and, above all, to believe in themselves. The following wonderful story is a powerful reminder of this.

One day a principal called in three teachers and said, 'You three are the finest in the system, so we're giving you ninety high-IQ students, to see what you can do with them.' By the end of the year the students achieved 30 per cent more than the other students in the school. The principal called the three teachers in and said, 'I've a confession to make. You didn't have ninety of the most promising students; we picked them at random.' The teachers naturally concluded that their exceptional teaching skills must have been responsible for the students' wonderful progress. 'I have another confession,' said the principal. 'You're not the brightest teachers either, your names were the first three drawn out of a hat.'

Why did those teachers, and their students, perform at such an exceptional level? Because they were given self-belief and encouraged to believe they could!

All good educators and communicators soon come to realise that real education and real communication begin when we are willing to start from where the other person *is*, rather than from where we would like them to be, and when we give them every encouragement to be the best they can be.

It was the writer Mark Twain who said, 'One compliment can keep me going for a whole month.' A word of encouragement can change a child's life. As the Bible says, 'Gracious words are a honeycomb, sweet to the soul and healing to the bones' (Prov. 16:24).

Keep it simple

So how do we put people before process? Often the answer is to be found in keeping things simple. Process has a way of overcomplicating things, clogging our path with 'shoulds' and 'oughts' and tripping us up with red tape.

Professor Vernon Bogdanor, Professor of Government at the University of Oxford, said, 'If one joins a cricket club, one does not expect to spend one's time discussing the club's constitution.' How succinctly put. Too much process and bureaucracy can leave us despairing. We wonder if anyone understands what we are trying to do. So much time and energy is wasted on form-filling, on checking up on others and their performance, on arranging, attending and writing up meetings. Yet as the life and example of Jesus of Nazareth show, our real responsibilities are with and alongside people. So often in our society it can appear that those who know the detail, who are conversant with the processes and who are able to source knowledge, are the ones to be trusted and relied upon – that is, until we discover otherwise.

The consultant strategist for one of the world's leading airlines was a Harvard-educated high-flyer who had always been top of his class. His success was based on the process of handing in good work to tutors, and now to his employers, then having the kudos of good marks and being highly regarded as a result. But this bright and hard-working young man was missing something.

The airline for which he was working was considering a vital deal with another international carrier, a potential merger which would have long-lasting effects. The young consultant strategist had done his research and knew the merger was a good idea. All he had to do was to convince the board of his arguments.

Sadly, when the time came, the board was not convinced, and the deal fell through.

What went wrong? The young strategist had presented an excellent paper to the board, after all. But he had been so busy concentrating on his paperwork that he failed to spend time with the members of the board, and in particular the chief executive and chairman, discussing and explaining the deal. Had he done so, he could have addressed their individual questions, doubts and concerns. In his efforts to perfect the process, he overlooked the need to put people first and failed to realise that real, lasting change does not come from impressive paperwork, however well worked out and presented, but happens one on one, one by one and then in partnerships.

Soon afterwards a competitor international airline from another country 'swooped' on the opportunity for a merger, which has since led to an impressive transatlantic partnership.

If only that young strategist had been less academic in his approach and taken more time and trouble with people rather than with the process, the history of our international airlines might have been be dramatically different.

There is, in our age, no more inspiring example of how to keep things simple than Mother Teresa of Calcutta. She always endeavoured to put people before processes, governmental or otherwise. When she received the Nobel Peace Prize she was asked by a leading world figure, 'What can we do to promote world peace?' Her answer was simply, 'Go home and love your family.'

Such a simple answer, so full of meaning. A good friend of mine, the much-respected author Charles Handy, co-founder of the London Business School, specialises in writing about organisational behaviour and management and he has a wonderful way of simplifying what fellow human beings have endeavoured to make complex. His books and speeches are regularly described as beacons of light in the gloaming, rather in the same manner that ships are steered safely through the swirling fog with the aid of lighthouses. One of Charles's most useful phrases is that of the 'irreducible minimum', asking each individual to look at their life in terms of their needs, possessions and aspirations, and reduce these to the essential basics. This is a wonderful clarifying exercise that I have found to be incredibly helpful, allowing me to re-evaluate my own personal needs and those of my family, and so to learn to live and work in a much more balanced way. Such an approach requires constant review, working out how much one needs to earn to make ends meet and then (and this can be delightfully surprising) what proportion of one's life one can give to other interests – not least being of use and service to others. 'Follow your heart' might be a useful way of summing up Charles's 'irreducible minimum'.

At a time when the number of civil servants across Western first-world democracies is on the increase, creating more and more overweighted bureaucracies, surely the time has come to call a halt and instead to begin to move things in the other direction, towards the irreducible minimum that will do enough to keep things flowing effectively and smoothly, but not interfere and hinder imagination and innovation.

Perhaps our leaders and our civil servants sometimes need to chuckle a little more, in the manner of the Dalai Lama, to take things more lightly and appreciate the opportunity to make them simpler than they have generally been to date. One of the by-products of overprescribing about how we should live our lives is that there is a danger people will no longer trust themselves or each other. Keeping prescriptive messages, rules and laws to a minimum indicates an inclination to trust people to do the right things, to know their own hearts and consult their own inner wisdom.

Jesus followed his heart, and if that meant breaking a rule to put a person first, then he did not hesitate. In his day the Sabbath was sacred, and no work of any sort was to be performed on that day. According to the strict letter of the Law, when Jesus healed the man with the shrivelled hand he was breaking the Sabbath. There were great cries of indignation: 'Is it lawful to heal on the Sabbath?' Jesus replied, 'If any of you has a sheep and it falls into a pit on the Sabbath, will you not take hold of it and lift it out? How much more valuable is a human being than a sheep! Therefore it is lawful to do good on the Sabbath' (Matt. 12:11–12).

For those who keep things simple, common sense and justice will always be the measure of what is right and what is not.

Despair and grief were the burden of a small group of church people in a conflict zone in Northern Ireland at the height of the troubles. So they decided to concentrate on prayer – not wordy prayers from a pulpit or a lectern, but in a small group, listening in and to the silence, allowing deep individual and collective emotions to surface and to be considered.

After several weeks this small group of Presbyterians began to grow. Prayer, silent and powerful, had become a community event.

> Are we weak and heavy laden,
> Burdened with a load of care?
> We should never be discouraged,
> Take it to the Lord in prayer.

One evening an old man stood up and said, 'We've simply got to cross the road.' He meant the abandoned no-man's-land of a highway between the Protestant and Catholic parts of the town. So sure was the old man in his conviction that he persuaded the others and, that very evening, they did indeed 'cross the road'. And what did they find? Their first stop was to knock on the door of the Roman Catholic church, where they were warmly welcomed with cups of tea and greeted with cries of, 'We've been praying all these months that you would cross the road!'

That simple action – getting up and walking across the road into the 'territory' of the other side – did what no amount of paperwork, theory, organisation or meetings could: it brought together two groups of people, in friendship instead of war. We would do well to pause and to remember with those good people from Northern Ireland that 'the power of prayer availeth and effecteth much'.

Those words would have struck a chord with St Columba on his journey across the sea from Northern Ireland to

Scotland, where he set up his abbey and monastery on the Island of Iona. It was from Iona that Columba's monks sailed in AD 563 in their tiny coracles to spread the gospel and bring civilisation to the mainland of Scotland – and well beyond. St Columba and his Celtic monks, more than 1,400 years ago, placed particular emphasis on people; everyone was to be a guest and to be made to feel at home, as it were, on a common shared journey.

These have been the founding principles of Columba 1400, our Community and International Leadership Centre on the Isle of Skye in Scotland, where the emphasis has been very much on people rather than on process. This has been especially valuable in the Head Teachers' Leadership Academies, where over 300 head teachers from the state sector, both primary and secondary, have taken time out to examine within themselves what it was that brought them into the teaching profession in the first place. In rediscovering their mission and passion, these head teachers have gone back to their schools, many of them in tough areas, and have looked beyond the process and bureaucracy of day-to-day school life and begun a new process of re-engagement. Some have been honest enough to suggest that certain ostensibly 'essential' papers crossing their desks have been purposefully ignored by them and that their 'non-returns' have somehow not even been noticed by the authorities! Time spent at Columba 1400 on the magical misty Isle of Skye has enabled them to reassess their life's motives and their desire to be of use and service to other people's children and so to put 'people before process'.

Deeply inspired, these head teachers have then gathered their senior management teams and a selection of pupils throughout the age groups and drawn them into an Ambassadors' Leadership Academy which has led to further Leadership Academies across the age groups and even into local feeder primary schools.

It is as if the scales of restrictions have been cast off collectively and these teachers' pure and admirable reasons for going into the teaching profession in the first place have been joyously rediscovered.

Perhaps this is also what is happening within many churches, where the strength and vision are being reshaped and rekindled in the smaller, more personal setting of house churches, and house or cell groups in established churches. It is almost as if the processes of church life have got in the way of serving the individual spiritual and personal needs of people, and that they are finding their own way of embracing the totality of life rather than the narrowness of a top-down way of worshipping and believing.

Putting people first

When Jesus of Nazareth, most definitely the master of the 'irreducible minimum' in his own life, entered the temple on a particularly busy trading day, he followed his heart. Something within told him that 'enough was enough'. Priorities had been turned upside down, trade and finance were taking the place of the daily needs of the sick and the sad, the poor and the lame and the unlovely, who felt neither able nor worthy to mount the steps of the temple.

In that moment Jesus knew what he had to do. Just as Jesus cleared the temple then, so we must clear the temples of our own lives. And when, after careful thought and prayer, we are ready to do this, there will be a fire burning in our hearts which tells us that now is the time to act.

Perhaps the first step towards putting people first is to have the courage to say no to those things which clog up your day, week or life.

- Are you involved in too many meetings?
- Are you writing reports about reports?

- Could you walk across the corridor and have a conversation, instead of sending a memo?
- Are you putting so much effort into making sure your children have the right uniforms and do their homework that you forget to listen to them when they need to tell you what matters in their lives?
- Are you so busy organising your life that you forget to sometimes stop and just enjoy it — to smell a rose, instead of worrying about how the garden looks?

We all forget, sometimes, how to put people before process, but when we get it right, life becomes richer, more satisfying and more worthwhile. With less organising and form-filling and more emphasis on our abiding common humanity, we can recognise that 'doing the correct thing' is not the same as 'doing the right thing'.

Mark Twain said, 'Always do the right thing; this will gratify some people and astonish the rest!' And if you ever doubt what the right thing is, in any situation, look for the choice that puts people first.

Reflections

There is a Native American saying which reminds us, 'In order to walk in someone's shoes, you first have to take off your own.' Look around you, take off your shoes, and try on those of someone who is close to you. This will bring understanding and compassion.

What would your 'irreducible minimum' be? How much clutter is there in your life, in your family or your organisation? What can you do to remove some of the clutter and concentrate on what really matters?

Do you really wish to embrace change, beginning first of all in yourself? Are you truly focusing on other people and their needs, as opposed to your own concerns? How prepared are you to follow your heart and see God's purposes in and through the goodness of other people?

'Go home and love your family,' as Mother Teresa would encourage you to do. Help them to follow their hearts. Every now and then, clean out the temples of your life and open the windows and doors of your attic – for when you let in the light of the Holy Spirit you shall be doing the 'right thing'.

Wisdom Before Knowledge

The point of philosophy is to start with something so simple as not to seem worth saying – and to end with something so paradoxical that no one will believe it!

(Bertrand Russell)

In today's world there seems to be a constant search for an intellectual answer to everything. If we have a problem, we think about how to solve it. If the problem is governmental, they set up a 'think-tank' to solve it. Our approach to the issues life throws up tends to be academic, analytical and scientific. We trust what we know, and we disregard anything that cannot be proven.

Our children are judged most often by their exam results and academic performance. We make value judgements about people according to the university they went to or the job they do. We love people who are bright, smart, clever, sharp. We love those who can rattle off reams of facts on *Mastermind*, *Brain of Britain* or countless other quiz shows. And we enjoy watching razor-tongued television interviewers berating those who do not have all the facts, or who get them wrong.

Of course knowledge is a wonderful thing, and those who know a great deal are rightly respected and rewarded. But the amassing of information and facts is not everything. Mr S. N. Goenka, the renowned teacher of Vipassana Meditation – a system which goes back thousands of years in India and is said to cure all ills – and founder of meditation centres around the world, claims that we spend far too much time in the Western world concentrating on learning and knowledge. In his view, and in the practice of much of the Eastern world, the desire to seek and recognise wisdom is far more vital and more significant in human interactions.

So what is wisdom? It is perhaps best described as the capacity to realise what is of value in life, to recognise the fundamental interconnectedness of all peoples and all things, and to make use of this recognition in making choices and decisions. A wise person is perceptive, listens well, observes much, always attempts to understand all aspects of a situation, and acts with care, discernment and insight.

In areas of complexity and perplexity, wisdom when rightly cultivated will quite quickly, and often surprisingly, strike us as being much more valuable and reliable than the possession of knowledge or facts alone. A wise person will use their knowledge with care, never boasting, belittling or judging others or behaving in a grandiose way, but rather carrying their knowledge lightly, using humour and compassion to bring about results, or change when it is needed.

Wisdom can be acquired with experience, as we learn from what life brings us. But it can also be cultivated through conscious effort. Some people seem to be born wise, but most wise people have learned and practised their skills. The best place to start is by understanding more about what wisdom really is, learning from wise people, and discovering how to cultivate the inner wisdom we all have.

Hidden treasure

Solomon, in the book of Proverbs, indicates that if you search for wisdom as for 'hidden treasure', then you will 'find the knowledge of God' (Prov. 2:4–5). For him wisdom is a spiritual concept, inextricably linked with a deep, inner connection to God. And so it was for Jesus, who said, 'Seek first [God's] kingdom . . . and all these things will be given to you as well'

(Matt. 6:33). As we have already considered, he also said, 'The kingdom of God [or heaven] is within you' (Luke 17:21 NIV). So we should look within, to find the goodness and love inside us, and there we will also find true wisdom.

Time and again we find Jesus commending and encouraging those who were prepared to search for wisdom as for hidden treasure. When the early disciples asked him about the pecking order of the eternal, saying, 'Who, then, is the greatest in the kingdom of heaven?' Jesus replied, 'Unless you change and become like little children, you will never enter the kingdom of heaven' (Matt. 18:1–3). He even went so far as to say, 'I praise you, Father . . . because you have hidden these things from the wise and learned, and revealed them to little children' (Matt. 11:25).

Jesus' references to little children indicate that he wanted us to find in ourselves those qualities that little children naturally have – openness, simplicity, love and warmth. A small child does not judge you on your clothing, gender, colour or wealth, but will respond only to the way you behave towards him or her. This basic wisdom is in all of us, but for many it has been covered over by all kinds of complications, as we learn to judge others not on who they are but on what they have or what they look like. What Jesus is telling us is to get back to basics, to keep things simple, to look at who people are, if we want to be wise.

Many of us have become too intent on the amassing of learning, wealth or possessions for their own sake, so that our barns are overflowing, rather in the manner of the rich young man whose life had been spent in the accrual of wealth. But it was not enough to have kept all the commandments since he was a boy. Jesus looked at him in a loving and kind way, saying, 'One thing you lack . . . Go, sell everything you have and give to the poor, and you will have treasure in heaven. Then come, follow me.' Then the young man's face fell and 'he went away sad, because he had great wealth' (Mark 10:21–22).

What Jesus was saying to his earliest disciples – and the message he left for us – was to be careful about becoming attached to possessions. There are far greater and more important things to do and be concerned about in this life, which are indeed much more satisfying than repaying a mortgage or sustaining the level of a bank account, however large or small. Wealth can become a barrier to spiritual openness and wisdom. Wise people know when they have enough to meet their essential needs and seek no more than that.

Many very rich people who have enjoyed making their money come to realise that there are indeed many more important things in life than wealth – and in any case, you cannot take it with you! This is when a spirit of philanthropy, the love of mankind, enables such people to feel released and recognise that it is indeed a much happier thing to give than to be intent on getting and receiving.

Bill Gates, one of the best-known businessmen in the world, became America's wealthiest man after he founded what became the giant Microsoft Corporation. For many years Bill enjoyed being at the helm of the company and creating software innovations, but in recent years he has made a significant shift. In January 2000 he stepped down as chief executive of Microsoft, taking on a part-time role in order to devote the majority of his energies to the Bill and Melinda Gates Foundation, which he set up with his wife to pursue philanthropic endeavours. Since then he has donated massive amounts of money to various charitable organisations and scientific research programmes, announcing his avowed intention to do all he can to reduce extreme poverty in the world and advance the availability of health care.

What Bill Gates has done is both wise and generous. Not content to sit back and enjoy a lifestyle of unimaginable luxury, he wants to feel that there is a purpose and a use for his wealth and that it can be used to benefit others.

The wonderful thing is that each and every one of us can experience what it is like to be philanthropic – that is, generous and giving. We may not have great wealth, but whatever we do have we can find something to give, and we can give of ourselves – our time, our effort and our love.

Jesus knew that what is important is to give what we can. When the poor widow went to the temple and shyly donated her mite – the currency of those days – Jesus watched her. He must have seen how humble she felt, alongside those who paraded their wealth and made a display of their gifts, and he said, 'Truly I tell you, this poor widow has put in more than all the others. All these people gave their gifts out of their wealth; but she out of her poverty put in all she had to live on' (Luke 21:3–4).

Jesus often directed his message towards those who had become arrogant and uncaring through the acquisition of privilege and possessions, reminding them, 'The fear of the Lord is the beginning of wisdom, and knowledge of the Holy One is understanding. For through wisdom your days will be many, and years will be added to your life. If you are wise, your wisdom will reward you; if you are a mocker you alone will suffer' (Prov. 9:10–12).

Such words touched the hearts of many who heard him, for he was telling them that any one of them could, like the generous widow, choose to take the wise path of humility, giving all that she could out of her deep love for God, which wisdom would bring its own rewards.

The importance of the spiritual

What Jesus made clear in so many of the things he said and did was that it is not possible to become wise without developing your spiritual dimension. This does not mean that atheists cannot be wise, for of course they can, but rather that, whatever your beliefs, you need a spiritual connection to the wonder, beauty and glory of this extraordinary world.

For so many in the world today and throughout history, especially those who are touched by the truth, clarity and insight of what Jesus taught, this higher connection is with God.

Some discover, or rediscover, the teachings of Jesus very simply, through a story or an enlightening experience, after earlier disillusion. You may have been damaged in some way in an earlier religious experience. Or you may have felt hurt by someone or something to do with the official churches and with what others call religion. With such damage and hurt comes the understandable desire to defend oneself and not to get involved with any 'religious nonsense'. In this way many of us close down to the third vital dimension of our lives, the spiritual, and decide to concentrate purely on what we can see, touch, handle and verify, combining the mental and the physical. But while such a reaction is entirely understandable, if this has been your experience I hope you will open your heart to new possibilities, for to live without spiritual connection is to live a poorer life.

Jesus was well aware of the desire for verifiable certainty in life, and indeed was often confronted by it. He told the parable of the Sower as a response to this (Matt. 13:3–9). In the parable a sower went out to sow seeds, but some fell by the wayside so that the birds devoured them, and some fell on stony ground, without much earth, sprang up quickly and were scorched by the sun, and because they had no root the plants withered away. Some fell among thorns and were choked by the thorns and bore no fruit. But some fell on good ground and did yield fruit, thirty-, sixty- or a hundredfold. Jesus ended the parable by saying, 'He who has ears, let him hear.'

What he meant, as he explained to his disciples later, was that the seeds in his story represented words, with he himself as the sower. Some people would ignore him, others would listen but soon forget, others would be 'choked' by their riches and material things. But some would hear his words, understand them, take them in, go forth and live according to the wisdom of their hearts, multiplying this wisdom by passing it on to others.

The challenge for all of us is to find the 'good soil' in ourselves, allow the words of wisdom spoken by Jesus to take root, and find the wisdom in our hearts so that we can be wise for ourselves and our own lives and for our children and our children's children.

Jean Vanier was only seventeen when he accompanied his mother to meet starving victims of the Holocaust. So shocked was he by the sight of these skeletal fellow human beings, and by the evidence of such human cruelty, that after a short career in the navy he studied philosophy in Paris. Through his friendship with a priest named Father Thomas Philippe, he became aware of the plight of thousands of people institutionalised with developmental disabilities. Jean Vanier felt led by God to invite two men to leave the institutions where they lived and share a small house in a French village with him. This first community eventually became known as L'Arche, after Noah's ark, and was to lead to the setting up of 130 other L'Arche communities around the world, where people with developmental disabilities and those who assist them share life together.

In 1971 he co-founded Faith and Light, an international movement where people with developmental disabilities, their family and friends meet regularly to discuss their hopes and difficulties, and to pray together. Vanier, who has been awarded numerous international prizes for his lifelong commitment to the care, well-being and independence of those with disabilities, points out that when confronted with human brokenness and weakness, people often find God, whose love is without limitation. Today there are over 1,400 Faith and Light communities around the world.

The shared wisdom of Jean Vanier has made a difference in the lives of countless people around the world – those with disabilities, their families and the many young people over the years who have chosen to help in L'Arche communities. He has taught the abiding wisdom of how people in need – in a society which so often excludes them – want not just generosity but relationship and communion, and how, as human beings, we all learn to hide our inner brokenness and vulnerability behind the impenetrable screens of our capacities and our power.

Let award-winning author and columnist Ron Ferguson take up the story:

> Jean Vanier's God is a vulnerable deity, one who slips incognito into the margins of human life, where people bleed and weep. In his life experience and in his reflections, he expresses a religion of the heart, one which embodies the theology of the second century theologian Irenaeus: 'The glory of God is a human being fully alive.'
>
> Vanier is an irreverently joyful prophet of our time . . . He offers an alternative vision of how to be religious. His L'Arche communities in India, with Hindu, Christian, Muslim and non-religious assistants, are fragile, hope-bearing signs of compassionate and respectful living.[1]

Jean Vanier is a tall man with a generous smile who radiates compassion, and his 'alternative vision of how to be religious' echoes that of Jesus, who showed us that love for other people is the foundation of wisdom and of joy.

In the New Testament, the letter of James says:

> Who is wise and understanding among you? Let them show it by their good life, by deeds done in the humility that comes from wisdom. But if you harbour bitter envy and selfish ambition in your hearts, do not boast about it or deny the truth. Such 'wisdom' does not come down from heaven but is earthly, unspiritual, demonic. For where you have envy and selfish ambition, there you find disorder and every evil practice. But the wisdom that comes from heaven is first of all pure; then peace-loving, considerate, submissive, full of mercy and good fruit, impartial and sincere. Peacemakers who sow in peace reap a harvest of righteousness. (Jas 3:13–18)

In his Bible translation *The Message*, Eugene Peterson, pastor, scholar, author and poet, paraphrases those final verses in more modern terms:

> Real wisdom, God's wisdom, begins with a holy life and is characterised by getting along with others. It is gentle and reasonable, overflowing with mercy and blessings, not hot one day and cold the next, not two-faced. You can develop a healthy, robust community that lives right with God and enjoy its results *only* if you do the hard work of getting along with each other, treating each other with dignity and honour. (Jas 3:17–18, *The Message*)

Wise for ourselves

To be wise in relation to other people, to do the hard work of getting along with others, we must be wise about ourselves. You cannot nurture and support others, be there for them, listen and give of your time and energy, if you are careworn and exhausted.

Jesus said to his disciples, 'Come with me by yourselves to a quiet place and get some rest' (Mark 6:31).

He recognised the great value of 'time out', a break from routine to pause, reflect and renew one's energies. This is particularly true when one faces dilemmas and choices. Very often it is only after a pause or a rest in a 'quiet place' that ways forward become apparent and clear and we are able to make decisions. With such time to pause, a beautiful view or a painting may touch the soul, the plot of a novel might encourage us to look deeper into the ongoing complexity of human life, or a resonant piece of music may describe the best of who we are and who we could yet become. Refreshed and inspired, we can then return to what we have to do with new insight and energy.

Perhaps you are going through some time of tension and indecision in your own life. You may feel torn, pulled in several directions, and long once again to feel in control. Certainly we all feel like this at times, and in those moments we can feel and hear the pulse of our hearts racing to the extent that our minds can become, as we say in Scotland, like mince! Heart pounding, head thumping, not sure of what to do – in those circumstances all the libraries in the world cannot help. It is only when we choose, with serenity in our hearts, to reset our compass and renew our sense of purpose and service, that we have truly found our inner wisdom.

In that way we can amass all our resources to enable us to become and to stay calm. Many have written and spoken of this extraordinary human ability within our souls. We all have it and can use and strengthen it in ourselves. Finding calm amid chaos, nurturing in ourselves the ability to stand back and detach, so that we can remain centred no matter what happens, this is the goal if we wish to cultivate wisdom.

The wise know that we are all flawed, that life itself is flawed, but that it is in those very flaws that we find hope, enlightenment and understanding.

Leonard Cohen, the Canadian poet, writer and musician, whose body of work is hugely influential, thoughtful and insightful, made and lost a fortune twice – once to his former manager, who misappropriated millions of dollars from him. Cohen, a deeply spiritual man, spent five years as a Zen Buddhist monk in the 1990s, retiring completely from performing. But, with no money left, he returned to performing in his seventies and found huge success all over again. In his moving song 'Anthem', he says:

> Ring the bells that still can ring,
> Forget your perfect offering,
> There is a crack in everything,
> That's how the light gets in.[2]

What Cohen is saying is that we can forget about perfection: we will not find it. But in the inevitable flaws – in ourselves, in life, in the world around us – we will find the 'light' of insight, optimism, love and connection.

The connection with others, so vital to us as human beings, is a potential source of great joy, not only for what we can do for others, but for what they can do for us. For the wise learn when to ask for help. It is not wise to struggle alone, just as it is not brave to remain isolated and refuse to ask those around you to help. In fact, it is often the braver choice to ask for help, for this means to admit to vulnerability, to the need for others, and to the fact that one is struggling to cope.

Such wisdom is beautifully encapsulated in the story of Cliff Schimmels, well-known American Baptist Professor of Education, speaker and author, who recalled, 'When I was young my dad had a team of horses. One day he said to me, "Son, would you like to drive?" So I took the reins. I was in control. I was driving. But the plodding bothered me, it was too slow. So I clucked the horses, Babe and Blue, along and they began to trot. Then Babe and Blue came up with a better idea. They decided that if they ran we would get home faster. Soon they were running as fast as I've ever seen horses run. As the prairie-dog holes whizzed by I concluded that we were in a dangerous situation, so I tried my best to slow down the runaway team. I tugged on the reins until my hands cramped. I cried and pleaded, but nothing worked. Old Babe and Blue just kept running. I glanced over at my dad and he was just sitting there, watching the world go by. By now I was frantic. My hands were cut from the reins, tears streaming down my face, frozen from the winter cold. Finally in desperation I turned to my dad and said, "Here, take the reins." Now that I am older and people call me Grandpa, I re-enact that scene at least once a day.'

What Cliff learned that day was that there comes a time when you simply have to ask for help. His father was wise enough to let him learn that through experience, when many another parent might have taken over before being asked. What stayed with Cliff was the powerful message that when the going gets too tough, help is at hand if you will only ask for it.

This is a simple truth that many have discovered through the power of prayer. We do not have to suffer alone, we can ask for help, and if we do so it will be given.

It is also through our connection with others that we discover what is of value and what is not, and learn to trust our own judgement. John Alexander Smith, Professor of Moral Philosophy at the University of Oxford, put this very succinctly when he said, in his 1914 opening lecture to his students, 'Nothing that you will learn in the course of your studies will be of the slightest possible use to you in later life – save only this: that if you work hard and intelligently, you should be able to detect when a person is talking rot. And that, in my view, is the main if not the sole purpose of education.'

How neatly and beautifully he put the message that there is more to life than knowledge and the mere amassing or processing of factual knowledge. A far more fundamental aspiration of education must be that constant search for wisdom which, in its simplicity, cuts through all the knowledgeable padding to the real essence of any issue.

What John Alexander Smith was pointing out was that to be wise, we need to be able to tell what is genuine, truthful and real from what is fake, dishonest and false. To be able to do this we need to trust ourselves and our own judgement – this was what he viewed as a worthy end result of education.

If we do not trust our own judgement, we cannot follow our hearts towards our true purpose.

The great Welsh Christian poet R. S. Thomas wrote:

> It is too late to start
> for destinations not of the heart.[3]

His moving words sum up so perfectly how important it is for us to do all that we do in life with heart. If we do not, then our spirits cannot soar.

My father was about to go up to Cambridge in 1939 when the war broke out. He deferred his place and went to war, becoming the youngest officer to return home from the beaches of Dunkirk in France.

At the end of the war he was assured that his place at university was still waiting and he was filled with excitement at the thought of finally taking up his studies. He had decided to become either a dentist or a minister of the church, and he was looking forward to following his heart to find out in which of these fields his future lay. But when he went to his father with the letter from Cambridge, confirming his place, my grandfather said, 'Surely you don't want to do that after all you've been through. Why don't you come and join me and your brothers in the family business?' Most people in post-war Britain would have told him that it was the 'right' thing, the sensible thing, to go into the family business with his father and brothers and in that moment, eager to please his father, he allowed himself to be swayed into that business career. Yet deep within he knew this was not the path he truly felt drawn to and he could never fully enjoy his work. The choice he made, despite a very happy family life, ultimately contributed to his early death through a devastating heart attack. His inner tension was unbearable, as we realised after his death, when we learned that, unbeknown to my mother, he had made several late-night visits to our minister in order to discuss whether or not he really had a vocation for the ministry.

We who loved him felt deeply saddened that he had not been able to fulfil that dream. He was a wonderful father, who gave us so much, and who would have made a gracious and inspiring minister.

In contrast, the following is a tale of another young man who returned from the same war.

A highly decorated marine returned home to the United States after the war, faced with a choice of career. A celebrated war hero and a very bright young man, he could easily have become a diplomat, a politician, a lawyer or a businessman, all careers leading to a high likelihood of success and a secure salary. Yet he could not make up his mind, for, by his own admission, there was an inner voice which seemed to be guiding him and to which he felt he had to listen.

One evening he went to a revue in his local community, towards the end of which a young blind girl came on stage to sing the song '*Que Sera, Sera*', '*Whatever Will Be, Will Be*'. As he listened to her beautiful voice, he finally realised what lay on his heart, and soon afterwards he took a job in the social work department of his local city. Not many years later he became head of social work for his home state. Ultimately, he became in the latter days of his career the chief advisor on social work to the President of the United States of America.

Those two war heroes, my father and the young US marine, would surely have understood what the celebrated New Zealand author and poet Joy Cowley had in mind in her book *Psalms Down Under* when she wrote this poem entitled 'Tension'.

> I am being pulled two ways.
> There is a voice in my heart
> which calls me to journey
> out there in deep waters,
> while another voice in my head
> tells me to stay close
> to a safe and familiar shore.
>
> The heart voice is like a strong tide
> drawing me to the infinite.
> The head voice moors me
> to a secure harbour
> of possessions and ideas.
>
> I know that the head voice
> comes from my human nature
> and is a part of my instinct
> for survival on this planet.

The voice is loud, and says
in a number of different ways,
'What about me? What about me?'

The voice of the heart is gentle
and as quiet as moonlight.
All that it says is, 'Come!'
but its pull is very strong
and my heart strains away from my head
in deep longing.

I know that there is a season
for waiting in safe harbours,
a time for material security,
for feeding the human self
with things and ideas of things.
What I pray for in this moment
is the gift of discernment.
May I learn to read the tide, and know
when to cast off the moorings
to sail those deep and uncharted waters
of God's infinite love.[4]

'God's infinite love', of which that beautiful poem speaks, is best found in the life and teachings of Jesus of Nazareth, whose profound wisdom enabled him to extract the essential from the trivial.

The bigger picture

While knowledge can inform us of the details of a situation, it is wisdom that allows us to see the bigger picture.

Perhaps it was this realisation that occasioned Robert Kennedy, US Attorney General, presidential candidate and younger brother of President Jack Kennedy, some four decades ago, to dismiss the use of mere facts such as figures on Gross National Productivity (GNP) to set the nation's priorities. In a speech given on the 18th March 1968 purportedly written by the economist Edgar Cahn, founder of Time Banks, Robert Kennedy said that such factual knowledge

> does not allow for the health of our children, the quality of their education, or the joy of their play. It does not include the beauty of our poetry or the strength of our marriages, the intelligence of our public debate or the integrity of our public officials. It measures neither our wit nor our courage, neither our wisdom nor our learning . . . it measures everything, in short, except that which makes our life worthwhile.

Small wonder, then, that so many of us turn away from news broadcasts or from party political pundits whose 'facts' very often prove to be overestimations of what is possible, leading ultimately to more broken promises as each electoral cycle rolls around.

When a government has lost its way or an organisation is at its wits' end, the default reaction is to set up a think-tank, a commission or an enquiry. However well intentioned the participants, the competitive urge among those who are perceived to be clever or learned – and yet may have very little experience of what is actually happening on the ground – can lead to what might be described as an 'academy of deliberators' with a veritable host of policy papers and guidelines, many of which are all too readily filed away without being read. All the while those responsible for delivery on the ground are only asking that people speak simply and authentically from the heart and not participate in horse-trading of politically inspired academic ideas.

In post-apartheid South Africa, Archbishop Desmond Tutu was one of those who saw the bigger picture – that reconciliation was the only way to bring together all sides in this nation of many parts.

Desmond Tutu, a humorous and bravely outspoken man, had always provided that rich seam of wisdom for others to consult and to rely upon during South Africa's long struggle towards release from apartheid. In the midst of all that was going on both inside and outside South Africa, throughout Nelson Mandela's imprisonment and 'long walk to freedom', Desmond Tutu was the quiet voice who spoke against the cacophony of those urging retribution and violence.

In the early years of the Rainbow Nation, following the lifting of apartheid, Desmond Tutu was one of those who set up the Truth and Reconciliation Commission, without which the nation would never have moved on. This commission was little short of a spiritual miracle. A mere factual knowledge of previous events would almost certainly have indicated that such a concept would be a disaster, but it was the spiritual wisdom of Desmond Tutu which led the way to ultimate triumph.

The Truth and Reconciliation Commission, first set up in 1990, was a court-like body in which witnesses who were identified as victims of human rights violations were invited to give statements about their experiences, and perpetrators of violence could also give testimony and request amnesty from both civil and criminal prosecution.

What happened in the Truth and Reconciliation Commission was often profoundly moving. Who could have foreseen the white Afrikaner confessing to a black widow that he had killed her husband, or a black 'terrorist' saying sorry for the hurt, violence and killing which he had caused – one asking forgiveness of the other and both receiving it.

In 1994, in an NPR interview, Desmond Tutu said,

We were made to enjoy music, to enjoy beautiful sunsets, to enjoy looking at the billows of the sea and to be thrilled with a rose that is bedecked with dew . . . human beings are actually created for the transcendent, for the sublime, for the beautiful, for the truthful . . . and all of us are given the task of trying to make this world a little more hospitable to these beautiful things.[5]

He saw the bigger picture, the beauty in the world around us and in the human soul, and knew that forgiveness was the only way forward. He had the wisdom that enables us to see above and beyond each and every apparent calamity or difficulty and to know, in the famous words of Julian of Norwich, that, 'All shall be well, and all manner of things shall be well.'

Julian of Norwich was a great medieval mystic and writer, who lived in a cell attached to St Julian's Church in Norwich, spending her days in contemplative prayer. Although she lived in a time of turmoil – she lived through the Black Death and several peasant revolts – her theology was optimistic. For Julian, suffering was not a punishment that God inflicted, as was the common understanding then. She believed that God loved and wanted to save everyone and spoke of God's love in terms of joy and compassion as opposed to law and duty. In her wisdom, Julian of Norwich held that, if we can only step back and see the bigger picture, then truly all will be well.

Building wisdom

From those who are wise, we learn that wisdom is a serious quality of inner strength and growth, and that it needs to be worked at. We need to store away and remember moments of wisdom, when they came to us and by whom they were inspired. Such moments will often happen when we least expect them.

It will be wisdom rather than the accumulation of facts and of knowledge that will inspire us to live our lives in good, rich, nurturing soil. Then, in our behaviours with others, reflecting our innermost intentions, we will be able to begin to understand what Jesus of Nazareth meant when he said to his disciples prior to his death, 'All this I have spoken while still with you. But the Counsellor, the Holy Spirit, whom the Father will send in my name, will teach you all things and will remind you of everything I have said to you' (John 14:25–26 NIV).

In this way Jesus was indicating to his earliest disciples, and to all those who would listen and follow since, that there is a higher pathway of wisdom which does indeed surpass all our human understanding.

Sometimes that higher pathway of wisdom will be given to us in the most unlikely and least expected ways. We may see something of beauty, hear a remark that resonates deeply within us, or remember a verse or a thought which somehow gives us the strength and confidence to continue. Take this quote, for instance, most often attributed to the French novelist Albert Camus:

> Don't walk in front of me, I may not follow.
> Don't walk behind me, I may not lead.
> Just walk beside me and be my friend.

In similar vein, I will never forget how, some years ago, our then eleven-year-old son Ruaraidh, while with us on a visit to Australia, slipped a note to his eldest sister Maggie. We were due to return to Scotland, leaving Maggie to begin a new life thousands of miles away from home. Ruaraidh's note read, 'Remember to run with your heart and not with your mind' – and she has.

Words of wisdom can soothe and comfort, uplift and impart courage, and there are none more inspiring or reassuring than those of Jesus of Nazareth when he said, 'Peace I leave with you; my peace I give you. I do not give to you as the world gives. Do not let your hearts be troubled and do not be afraid' (John 14:27).

Such words are a gift which enables us to live with peace in our hearts. Such peace finds its beginning and its end in the wisdom of the one who loved us so much that he was prepared to give his life on a cross and die for us; the one who in his earthly life was prepared to risk the ridicule of those who knew their facts so well and yet whose souls were so undernourished.

The wonderful American writer Mitch Albom, quoting his professor Morrie Schwartz in his book *Tuesdays with Morrie*, wrote:

> Remember what I said about finding a meaningful life? Devote yourself to your community around you, and devote yourself to something that gives you meaning and purpose. Status will get you nowhere. Only an open heart will allow you to float equally between everyone.

Knowledge has a curious habit of encouraging us to see life as an end in itself. Wisdom, on the other hand, sees life as a journey, a lifelong process of learning, and a great eternal adventure.

Reflections

Are you ready for a new mindset? Are you prepared on occasion to go against the constant search for factual knowledge and to look for 'hidden treasure', the wisdom for each and every situation? Such wisdom will encourage you to find your freedom in simplicity and to avoid too many attachments, material or personal.

If you run with your heart and not just with your cautious mind, you will be able to 'hand over the reins'. And if you listen and learn in your prayers, you will hear God's voice 'in a breath of silence'.

Take time out from your busy life to rest, renew and connect with the beauty of this wonderful world. You will be better able to be there for others.

Integrity Before Politics

The way you have infused the knowledge about human
beings and the society we live in with the Christian
spirit, this way of yours has a great liberating force.

(International visitor to Columba 1400)

Mahatma Gandhi was once asked, 'Mr Gandhi, what do you
think of Western civilisation?' He paused for a short while and
then replied, 'Now that would be a very good idea!'

Everyone enjoyed the joke, but Gandhi, the leader of India's
non-violent resistance to British rule, was clearly intimating,
in his own humorous and gentle way, that he did not think the
West was civilised at all. And perhaps that was, in part at least,
because we in the West rely so heavily on politics.

Of course every nation needs politics, and politicians. But
I am talking about politics in its worst and wider sense – that
is, dealings which are self-serving often hide an ulterior motive
behind a declaration of honesty, and manipulate others. In
every sphere of modern life there are those who scheme, who
are crafty, who play games to get their own way, or who declare
one agenda but have another hidden agenda that they are
pursuing.

This kind of politics can be very subtle and can even appear
well meaning. It can be hard to spot, although ultimately we
always know when we have been on the receiving end.

Just as a politician on the hustings will make claims and
promises, only to declare later that it was not their fault if the
promises were broken, so a political 'player' in any field may
promise what he or she knows may not be possible to deliver.

123

In contrast, integrity is about being sound, upright and honest. When there is integrity, what you see is what you get, what is promised is what is delivered and dealings are characterised by fairness, consideration and honesty.

The third of our principles is integrity before politics, because I believe it is vital that we all put decency and honesty before self-seeking ends. Where there is integrity people feel respected and considered. Of course there are politicians with integrity; the two are not mutually exclusive. Many upright and honest people have done their best to achieve good within the world of politics and elsewhere. But sadly there are many people who do not act with integrity, and for whom dubious ends are justified by even more dubious means.

It was the late George MacLeod, founder of the ecumenical Iona Community, who, when asked if he believed in miracles, replied, 'If you don't believe in miracles, then I wish you a continuingly dull life!' Of course miracles can and do happen, and never more so than when politics are put aside and people of integrity act with their hearts and consciences.

Greed and mediocrity

Cliff Morgan, the celebrated Welsh international rugby player who went on to become head of BBC Radio 4 Sport, was speaking a few years ago at a star-studded international sporting gala. The diners were expecting a series of amusing sports anecdotes, so they were stunned when Cliff began by saying, 'The problem with society today is the lack of inspirational leadership. And that problem is twofold; first of all it is greed and secondly it is mediocrity.'

As Cliff spoke, many were struck by what this sparkling and intelligent sportsman was saying. The news at that time was full of the corruption scandals of WorldCom and Enron in the United States. And, as became clear soon afterwards, we were heading for a worldwide recession and Britain would soon be in the grip of the credit crunch which in so many people's eyes was caused by the greed of bankers.

During those dark days it was almost as if greed and mediocrity had been allowed to predominate to such an extent that all courage and integrity had simply moved out of the boardrooms of the banks and the financial institutions and governments of our world.

That crisis caused many people to re-evaluate their lives and priorities and to consider the balance of politics and integrity. All of us know that when there are problems in our personal or professional lives, very often the root of them is grounded either in our own greed and mediocrity, or in the greed and mediocrity of others.

If we allow greed and mediocrity to prevail in our business lives, then we may be tempted to join the ranks of the tired and weary and so to rely ever more on processes as opposed to the indomitable power of the human spirit. We will find ourselves treating people as objects towards an end, rather than putting people first.

And if we show greed and mediocrity in our family and personal lives, then we are failing those we care about most.

Lord Sacks, the Chief Rabbi of the United Hebrew Congregation of the Commonwealth, when commenting in the earliest days of the credit crunch, indicated that he had found great consolation in his Old Testament studies and reflections. He had once again realised that for the people of the Old Testament, 'It was only in the famines that they realised what the feasts were all about.'

I mentioned Lord Sacks's reflection to a leading female financial expert and investment analyst, to which her unthinking reply was, 'And I only wish we could get back to the feasts!' When I suggested that perhaps Lord Sacks had something else in mind, she replied, 'Yes, of course I see what he means.

When I think about it now, we only did what we did because we thought that everybody else was doing it.'

When I reflected on that phrase 'everyone else was doing it', it took me back to my days as a headmaster when a pupil, challenged or confronted about some particular action, or lack of action, gave the usual rather feeble response, 'I thought it was OK . . . because everyone else was doing it.'

If we lose our sense of individual responsibility, we are like sheep, blindly following one another, and this is the root of mediocrity. Only when we think and act for ourselves, following what we know and believe to be right, can we rise above mediocrity. It is up to each one of us to speak out, for justice and for truth, for the good of all of us.

A time of famine affords us the opportunity to reappraise the excesses of our lives, to re-evaluate that which is truly important, lasting and good, and in this sense it is a blessing.

The prophet Isaiah said,

For Zion's sake I will not keep silent,
for Jerusalem's sake I will not remain quiet,
till her vindication shines out like the dawn. . .
The nations will see your vindication. . .
you will be called by a new name
that the mouth of the Lord will bestow.
(Isa. 62:1–2)

That ancient prophetic passage perhaps describes 'integrity before politics' in a nutshell. When we find our inner voice, we become empowered to find the best opportunities and occasions within which to express our love, our joy, our peace, our patience, our kindness, our courage and our integrity. According to Isaiah, we will be given a new name, an inner precious name of knowing who we are and what we stand for, day by day becoming more fully human and more fully alive to what God in his wisdom has called each one of us to be and to do.

When John F. Kennedy became President of the United States of America he had no idea that he would shortly be called to deal with the Cuban missile crisis. In September 1962, the Cuban and Soviet governments placed nuclear missiles in Cuba. When US military intelligence discovered the weapons, the US government sought to do all it could to ensure their removal. The crisis is generally regarded as the moment at which the Cold War came closest to a nuclear war. The crisis ended on 28 October 1962, when President Kennedy and the United Nations Secretary-General reached an agreement with the Russians to dismantle the missiles in exchange for a no-invasion agreement.

This was an extraordinarily testing time for President Kennedy, but for the sake of his people, and for the peace of the world, he did not rest in his fight for peace. His courage and integrity through the high-stakes politics of the day were encapsulated when he addressed the American people, saying, 'The Chinese use two brush strokes to write the word "crisis". One brush stroke stands for danger, the other for opportunity. In a crisis, be aware of the danger – but recognise the opportunity.'

This applies to anyone facing a crisis. Any testing situation, alongside whatever pressures and difficulties it holds, will present an opportunity to act with integrity and to do the right thing.

Doing the right thing often means speaking the truth, however unpalatable that may be for some. It was another American, the historian and author Henry Brooks Adams, who said, 'I would rather starve and rot and keep the privilege of speaking the truth as I see it, than hold all the offices that capital has to give from the presidency down.'

Stand up for those things which matter

We never can tell when our courage and integrity will be called to account amid the maelstrom of the politics of our daily personal and working lives. As Martin Luther King famously said, 'Our lives begin to end when we fail to stand up for those things which matter.'

It is not easy to put yourself on the line, but a marvellous liberating force can come into the heart and mind when you have the courage to stand up and be counted. In that moment you know what truly matters, and that all else comes second. And as you are liberated from fear, so others are liberated from fear as well, by your brave and honest actions.

Confucius said, 'To know what is right and not do it is the worst cowardice.' Yet we have all been cowards at one time or another and we all have to deal with the 'if onlys' in our lives – those times when we wish we had said or done something which we know in retrospect would have made all the difference to ourselves, or to our family life, or the lives of many throughout our organisation, community or even country. Who was it who said, 'Hell on earth is another way of expressing missed opportunity'?

What was it that held us back? Was it fear, uncertainty, anxiety? Whatever it was, we promise ourselves that next time we will do things differently. And we can – once the decision is made and is clear in our heart.

When, as a promising young lawyer, I realised I wanted to be a minister, I dreaded disappointing my newly widowed mother, who was intent on my future career as a lawyer. My father had just died and I was afraid that the news would break my mother's heart. I found myself thinking, praying and worrying until I came across Jesus' words in Luke's Gospel, words which have remained with me ever since in all 'knee-knocking' moments.

> They will deliver you to synagogues and prisons, and you will
> be brought before kings and governors . . . But make up your
> mind not to worry beforehand how you will defend yourselves.
> For I will give you words and wisdom that none of your adver-
> saries will be able to resist or contradict. (Luke 21:12–15)

When I read that passage, I was able to let go of my fears and
trust that, when the time came, I would know what to say to
my mother.

If those words were encouraging to me in a personal crisis
when my own integrity was being tested against the more sensible
politics of the day, then how encouraging must such assurances
have been to those who heard Jesus' message at that time.

His words were powerful, and even more so when the time
came for him to face the ultimate test. There can be no finer
proof of a man's words than to see them lived out, and indeed
that came to pass. Not many months later, Jesus was called
to demonstrate how the integrity of his message came before
the politics of the day. When he was arrested by the religious
authorities, the high priest questioned him about his teaching. It would have been easy then to indulge in some political
chicanery with clever words of avoidance. Yet Jesus chose the
high road.

> 'I have spoken openly to the world,' Jesus replied. 'I always
> taught in synagogues or at the temple, where all the Jews
> come together. I said nothing in secret. Why question me? Ask
> those who heard me. Surely they know what I said.'
>
> When Jesus said this, one of the officials nearby slapped
> him in the face. 'Is this the way you answer the high priest?'
> he demanded.
>
> 'If I said something wrong,' Jesus replied, 'testify as to what
> is wrong. But if I spoke the truth, why did you strike me?'
> (John 18:20–23)

This is a powerful cameo of how Jesus lived out his life and faith with complete integrity amid the petty political wrangling of the time.

The integrity of the life, death and resurrection of Jesus has provided a bedrock of strength and reassurance for many who have challenged the status quo. And when brave men and women stand up for the things that matter and give voice to those who cannot speak for themselves, then greed and mediocrity retreat into the shadows. Such people give light and encouragement to all those around them.

> Paul Moore trained as a barrister and, after seven years spent practising law, in 2002 he moved to HBOS (Halifax Bank of Scotland), where he was head of Group Regulatory Risk, with formal responsibility for the bank's compliance with the Financial Standards Authority's regulations. In November 2004 Moore was dismissed by HBOS chief executive officer Sir James Crosby. Moore claimed this was because he had repeatedly warned his bosses about the bank's reckless and excessive consumer lending. 'I felt like a man in a rowing boat trying to stop the *Titanic* heading for the iceberg,' he says.
>
> He sued HBOS for unfair dismissal and the bank settled his claim for over half a million pounds. Moore agreed to a non-disclosure agreement as part of his settlement, but he felt deeply unhappy with this and agonised about what to do for a long time. A committed Catholic, he said that he had always been guided by his faith, conscience and moral code. Eventually he decided, after many sleepless nights and long discussions with his wife, to speak out. This would mean giving back the money, but he felt the issue was simply too important; he had to tell the truth. On 10 February 2009 he submitted evidence to the UK's Treasury Select Committee which was investigating risks taken by UK banks in the lead up to the credit crunch. As a result of Paul Moore's evidence Sir James Crosby, who had left HBOS to become deputy chairman of the FSA, resigned.

Afterwards Paul Moore said, 'I feel at peace with myself. I feel like David taking on Goliath, and like David I'm running towards Goliath and not keeping my mouth shut. Sir James is a good person, but like so many in the banking industry he was afflicted by a form of blindness to what was happening.'

As Paul Moore found, sometimes it can be incredibly hard to stand up for what is right when so many would rather you kept quiet. In the end he answered only to his conscience, a sure sign of his deep integrity.

A *little bit of heaven*

Sometimes it takes enormous determination and integrity to bypass all the political obstacles and follow a dream. It was George Bernard Shaw who said, 'You see things that are, and you say "why?" But I dream of things that never were and I say "why not?"' The people who say 'why not?' in this life and go for it are the ones who are willing to wade through the river of politics to reach the other shore – and achieve their goals. For them 'tomorrow is the first day of the rest of our lives'. Their energy and enthusiasm may wane from time to time, but they are never lost. In the words of the Abba song:

> I have a dream, a song to sing
> To help me cope with anything
> If you see the wonder of a fairy tale
> You can take the future even if you fail
> I believe in angels
> Something good in everything I see
> I believe in angels
> When I know the time is right for me
> I'll cross the stream – I have a dream.[5]

In the mid-nineteenth century a young nurse named Florence Nightingale had a dream, and over the ensuing years she literally transformed dingy, dangerous, underperforming hospitals into places of hope and healing. She bravely accepted the challenge of upgrading hospital standards, improving patient care, enhancing sanitation and promoting nursing education. She faced many challenges and took them head on. First of all she overcame her mother's bitter opposition to her becoming a nurse. Then she achieved all that she did despite suffering from an illness which must have made life very difficult. And in addition she refused to marry, afraid that it might interfere with her nursing.

In her twenties Florence wrote in her diary, 'God called me in the morning and asked me would I do good for him alone without reputation.' And that is what she did, and continued to do, for the rest of her life.

In the course of her long career, she came across unimaginably petty politics at all levels, as she fought to establish better standards in patient care and to set up better training for nurses. Yet no matter what she faced, she was deeply committed to meeting the challenge of caring for those who were injured, sick and dying – she could do none other, for her heart of integrity was filled with love and compassion for her fellow human beings.

During the Crimean War, Florence Nightingale and her contingent of trained nurses saved many lives. When ill health forced her to return home to England, she was confined to her bed. The political authorities of the day were relieved, thinking that might be the end of her interference. Not so, for this brave soul somehow managed, now aged forty, to establish the Nightingale School and Home for Nurses in London. From her bed she created a medical revolution and continued to mastermind and direct those efforts until her death at the age of ninety!

Florence Nightingale came from a well-to-do family and could have chosen a cosseted lifestyle, yet she followed her heart and rose above the shortsighted politicians and persuasive arguments of the day. Her strength and her vision eased the pain of many, to the extent that she has ever since been recognised as the founder of nursing as a real profession, one of the most noble and respected throughout the world. Indeed, Florence Nightingale 'brought a little bit of heaven to earth' for her patients then and since.

Another remarkable woman who brings 'a little bit of heaven to earth' is Camila Batmanghelidjh, the founder of the charity Kids Company. Camila, an Iranian psychotherapist, spends her life looking out for and helping young, mainly Afro-Caribbean, people in parts of south London to realise their true potential.

Camila, who raises millions of pounds a year to fund her charity, has set up shelters literally underneath the arches of a railway, where young people can go and talk through their deepest fears and anxieties, a process headed towards realising their innermost hopes and aspirations.

In a speech at the Centre for Social Justice in London, Camila pointed out that in 1968 there were only nine drug deaths per annum in the United Kingdom and such is the current acceleration of drug-related crime that in her view, 'Young people are succeeding in breaking down the rest of us.' 'There are', she said, 'some deep humanitarian questions to be answered amidst an emotional and spiritual crisis needing to be addressed.' And then with typical courage and honesty she said, 'When the politicians have moved on, it is people like you and me who come out and make things happen.'

And so it is. Thank God that no amount of politics will ever extinguish the dignity and dynamism of the human spirit – or its intrinsic integrity. There will always be those of us who, through the serenity of our hearts, the purpose of our souls and in true service, realise that when we put people before process and wisdom before knowledge, our integrity will rise above mere politics and lead us to choose the more difficult, but ultimately the more fulfilling pathway.

When St Paul wrote to his fellow Christians in Ephesus, he was going through some tough times. His beliefs had been severely tested and he had been tortured; he had been ill and imprisoned. Yet amid his own suffering he was able to write to his friends in Ephesus, encouraging them, in his words, to 'put on the full armour of God'. He went on to say:

> Our struggle is not against flesh and blood, but against the rulers, against the authorities, against the powers of this dark world and against the spiritual forces of evil in the heavenly realms. (Eph. 6:12)

His advice in such circumstances was clear and to the point.

> Therefore put on the full armour of God, so that when the day of evil comes, you may be able to stand your ground, and after you have done everything, to stand. Stand firm then, with the belt of truth buckled around your waist, with the breastplate of righteousness in place, and with your feet fitted with the readiness that comes from the gospel of peace. In addition to all this, take up the shield of faith, with which you can extinguish all the flaming arrows of the evil one. Take the helmet of salvation and the sword of the Spirit, which is the word of God. And pray in the Spirit on all occasions with all kinds of prayers and requests. (Eph. 6:13–18)

Those words of St Paul have proved a tremendous source of encouragement to generations of men and women going through hard times, when their integrity has been questioned and tested against the more pragmatic and seemingly easier political choices.

This was the experience of a much respected Edinburgh minister who had tremendous difficulties night after night in the youth club that he ran for local youngsters. There was one young tearaway who succeeded in rubbing everyone up the wrong way, from fellow club members to the leaders and several parents as well. At the end of one club night a gathering of leaders, parents and members waited behind to speak to the minister and tried to put pressure on him, telling him that the club would have to close unless he excluded the young tearaway who had been causing so many problems.

A deep inner integrity called the minister to defend that young tearaway, to continue to spend more time with him and his family and to encourage the club leaders (whom he believed should have known better) to live up to their calling and to do the same. Although far from perfect, things began to get better, until the young tearaway boy finally finished school and left the youth club. What no one could have known at the time was that this young tearaway would one day become the first Scot in history to stand on the top of Mount Everest. His name was Dougal Haston.

If the minister had given in and excluded Dougal, the young lad might have taken a very different path in life, believing himself to be someone who could not fit in, or who was not wanted. The minister's firm stand, in the face of opposition, showed faith and belief in the youngster, and he backed up that faith by spending time with Dougal and instilling confidence in him.

Every one of us can look around and see someone for whom things might be different if they had someone who believed in them, who would listen, offer support, have faith and give encouragement. Every one of us can, with a little integrity, make a real difference to someone else's life.

Find connections

Sometimes differences and divisions are creations of our own minds and of the way in which we have been brought up. There can be great joy in discovering, despite apparent difference and division, that you are actually on the same track or engaged in the same search as someone else.

During a recent Leadership Retreat with a senior team from a large educational organisation, I found myself paired up with the chief executive for a coaching session. On the surface we had little in common. When we began to explore our respective childhood backgrounds we discovered, to our surprise, that we had been brought up a mile or so away from one another, in a ship-building town in the west of Scotland. Not only had we been brought up near each other, but we were exactly the same age and had both lost our fathers when we were only nineteen. It was extraordinary to reflect that we must have been going through the same sadness at the same time, just a short distance apart.

As we carried on talking we found we had even more in common, despite our very different family backgrounds. When I asked him, 'What has been your greatest passion in life?' he said, 'Social justice.' My answer to the same question was, 'Social responsibility.' As we talked, we discovered so many views and beliefs in common that we began to feel that together we could change the world!

That experience, of meeting and working with someone who, on the face of it, came from a different background and had made different life choices, was profound. It reminded me that to judge someone on outer appearances is to miss the possibility of finding out who they really are, and of making a deep and meaningful connection.

Several summers ago, I was invited by the Jewish and Hindu members of a multifaith pilgrimage to the remote Isle of Iona in Scotland to conduct a service. Iona is the resting place of the sixth-century Irish prince who became St Columba and from whose monasteries civilisation spread across Scotland. My first reaction to such an invitation was to indicate that I had a prayer service in mind, in order to be as open and accepting as possible of all faiths and traditions in our party. Yet the members of the pilgrimage insisted that I offer Holy Communion, and I gladly agreed.

When the time came, many of us were deeply moved, for not only did the Christians of various denominations come forward to receive the sacraments, but the Jews, the Muslims and the Hindus came forward to receive a blessing.

Hardly a word was spoken as we made our way from Iona Abbey to the jetty for the short boat trip to the *Hebridean Princess* ferry, anchored offshore. A deep sense of peace which passes all our human understanding had settled perceptibly over each one of us. Something truly remarkable had happened in all our lives.

When I look back on that magical service of Christian Communion, I recognise that it would not have taken place but for the persuasion and insistence of those of other faiths within our party. What does this tell us? Both in private and in the full glare of our Westernised first-world democracies we have become rather timid; we are shy about owning up to our heritage, to where we have come from. Perhaps 'political correctness' has gone so far that we find it easier not to be true to ourselves and our beliefs and so to avoid giving possible offence to others. Our presumption is often that they might take exception to our thoughts and beliefs and we tend to adopt a philosophy of peace and harmony at all costs.

The reality, as we found on Iona, can be very different. The encouragement to celebrate Communion, coming from people of other faiths, woke up the Christians present to the precious reality of their faith and practice. More than that, it encouraged some beautiful discussions, full of peace and harmony.

Martin Luther King once said, at the height of his reconciliation work, 'No one can believe how powerful prayer is, and what it is able to effect, but those who have learned it by personal experience.'

When you say your prayers with courage and integrity and hold nothing back, there arises within your heart a sense of freedom to become who you are and who you were meant to be, and to accept others for who they are, welcoming both differences and similarities. No wonder the psalmist was able to write, 'I run in the path of your commands, for you have set my heart free' (Ps. 119:32).

Cultivate integrity

Each one of us is a special child of God, a unique human being within whose soul there is a core of goodness and integrity. Our life's journey is an opportunity to eradicate the 'if onlys' that lead to regret and personal disappointment.

We are individual creations, who come into this world with a clean sheet; it is only the markings and jottings, very often of other people's persuasions and prejudices, that form the colour in the shapes of our life and thinking. Cast your mind back for a moment, give yourself a clean sheet and choose selectively what is good, right and true for you and for your conscience.

Albert Einstein said, 'Try not to become a man of success but rather try to become a man of value.' William Shakespeare put the same sentiment this way, in *Hamlet*: 'To thine own self be true, and it must follow, as the night the day, thou canst not then be false to any man.' This is the basis of integrity and of being a person of value – complete honesty with yourself and the courage to stick to what you believe to be the right path, even if this path appears to lead you away from apparent 'success'. To do this we must sometimes apply a rigorous self-appraisal and let go of any self-deceit, avoidance and denial. It is worth the effort, because when we do, we discover our own strength and courage.

All the mistakes, the 'if onlys', the moments when we might have done better, can weigh us down, like stones in our pockets. So reach for your integrity, and deal with those stones, so that you can move forward feeling lighter and easier in your heart.

Is there something in your personal or family life that requires the integrity of a straight answer or a pertinently addressed question? Is there someone you know at work who is being bullied or victimised verbally or, worse still, physically harassed, and you know that you have it within you to stand up for that person and be counted? Are you carrying a burden of guilt or regret and have for some time avoided that other person or situation in order not to be found wanting? Do you need to make amends to someone you have hurt? Perhaps the time has come to act, to drop any pride and arrogance and to 'cross the road' in humility and in mutual self-respect, to apologise wholeheartedly, offer a hand in reconciliation, stand up for someone who needs us, or simply let go of guilt and regret.

When you are able to do these things, you become a bigger person. You leave behind small-mindedness, meanness, pettiness, spite and revenge, and begin to see the good in everyone, and that everyone deserves a chance in life, truthfulness and respect from others. And you learn to clear the debris – political and otherwise – from your life and to hold fast to your clear intent and purpose.

In 1942, in the darkest days of the Second World War, every American soldier dreamed of being invited to join Easy

Company. Such an assignment was by no means 'easy', hence the irony of the name. The company was formed in Atlanta, Georgia with the specific aim of being the crack outfit whose soldiers would be the very fittest and best for what, two years later, history was to call D-Day. Had that brave company of men not been ready when the time came, the history of the world as we know it, not least in Europe, might have been very different indeed.

Stephen Ambrose, in his marvellous account which became an award-winning book and TV mini-series, *Band of Brothers*, told of how Easy Company was formed and trained in the hills of Georgia. The regime was tough, the expectations were high and anyone who was not true and loyal to the core purpose did not make it. The term 'chickenshit' was used to describe anything which got in the way of their ultimate purpose. And so they reached and exceeded their objectives.

I have told the story of Easy Company in conferences and leadership retreats and then asked the gathering, 'How much "chickenshit" is there in your life or in the life of your family, your business, organisation or profession?'

This has led to some honest and profound self-appraisal, which in turn has led to real benefits and, in some cases, to new ways of doing things.

In many cases those running an organisation have asked themselves, of each member of staff, 'Why did we hire that person, and what are they contributing to the organisation?' And they have often found that, without anyone noticing, a whole mound of 'chickenshit' has got in the way of people carrying out the work for which they were hired, and that within their organisation process has predominated over people, knowledge has appeared to conquer wisdom and politics has got the better of integrity.

The realisation of this presents a wonderful opportunity to clear out the debris, shift the 'chickenshit' and start afresh with new priorities.

Abraham Lincoln, one of the most distinguished and valiant presidents the United States has seen, summed up his philosophy of life with beautiful simplicity when he said, 'I never had a policy; I have just tried to do my very best each and every day.'

What better guide could there be for each of us to take with us through daily life? And as we do so, the power of the Holy Spirit will be with us, within us and alongside us in a deep sense of unbroken spiritual continuity. In that way we shall experience life in all its fullness and no matter what the world may think or say or throw at us, we will be able to stand up, look the world in the eye and love, laugh and live.

Reflections

Is there greed and mediocrity within your personal and working life? It is so easy to criticise others for these ills of society to which we may unwittingly be contributing ourselves – a time of 'famine' is a good time to clean out the stables of our own lives.

What are the 'if onlys' of your life and where might courage and integrity require you to 'cross the road' in humility and self-respect? When others have said to you, 'Why?', have you taken the opportunity to say, 'Why not?'

Miracles can and do happen, particularly when we are prepared to stand up for what we know to be good and true. Differences and divisions can, with courage and integrity, become shared purposes and commitments. How can we keep silent if our lives begin to end when we fail to stand up for those things which matter? Think carefully about those people and situations where a word in time from you could make all the difference.

The Three Qualities

Ancient literature reminds us of how men and women in the past have coped with and come through difficult circumstances, searching for those qualities and characteristics that have stood the test of time – qualities which mean that whatever the 'tsunamis' of a particular time or generation may be, the human spirit has always bravely endured.

I believe there are three qualities which stand out most of all as those necessary to our survival and spiritual growth. These were summed up by St Paul in his moving and beautiful letter to the Corinthians. Paul had established a Christian community in Corinth, Greece and was concerned that the Corinthians were quarrelling among themselves. Towards the end of a long letter pleading for unity, he wrote, 'And now these three remain: faith, hope and love. But the greatest of these is love' (1 Cor. 13:13).

St Paul was right. When all else fails us, if we have these three qualities, then we can survive anything, rebuild what has fallen, endure what must be endured.

In our journey together so far we have spent time considering three wisdoms and how the essences of serenity and purpose can enable us to discover, perhaps for the first time in our lives, who we really are, why we are here and where and to whom we are called to be of service.

With those wisdoms deeply embedded in our hearts, we become stronger in standing up for those principles which we know and believe to be true, right and lasting. No longer will process come before people, or knowledge before wisdom, or politics before integrity.

It is when we reflect on the occasions when we have failed to embrace and embody those principles that we recognise more clearly than ever before how much we need the qualities of *faith*, of *hope* and of *love*. At the end of the day, if only those three remain, then our need for them and our desire to embrace them becomes all the stronger.

These three qualities, which are so fundamental to the strength of the human spirit and to what it is to be human, are ultimately the bedrock of all else in our lives – which is why, in our journey together, I have saved the best until last. In their divine simplicity they are all that we need in order to survive the darkest hours of our lives, to nurture ourselves and others, to grow in wisdom and understanding, and to give generously of our time and ourselves.

Faith

If you are facing in the right direction, all
you need to do is keep walking.

(Ancient proverb)

Faith is that which sustains our spirit when all else has gone.
When we have faith we know that all is as it should be with us,
and that no matter what we must face, we will come through
and be stronger for it. Faith keeps us holding on when we are
tempted to give up. With faith, we can trust in ourselves, in
others, and in God, the higher power that will lead us forward
and give us the strength to survive.

It is faith that Rudyard Kipling was referring to when he
wrote, in the poem 'If':

> If you can force your heart and nerve and sinew
> To serve your turn long after they are gone,
> And so hold on when there is nothing in you
> Except the Will which says to them: 'Hold on!'

Faith is about holding on and keeping on, even when the road
ahead is filled with fears and doubts. Faith is the certainty that
is left to us when all else is uncertain. And it is faith that helps
us to treasure people and health more than possessions and
power.

Faith, in many people's minds is most often associated
with religious belief. Faith in God has enabled many of the
great figures of history to achieve extraordinary things and
to endure the unendurable. However, faith is not exclusively

religious. It is a quality of spirit which marks out all those who believe in themselves and in others, in rightness, goodness and justice. It is faith that makes us optimistic in the face of incredible odds, which keeps us keeping on when otherwise we might lose heart and which often allows us to achieve the seemingly impossible.

Think, for instance, of Lance Armstrong, one of the greatest cyclists of all time who, in overcoming the removal of a brain tumour and testicular cancer, went on to win six consecutive Tour de France races. Lance said:

> Without faith we are left with nothing but an overwhelming sense of hopelessness every single day, and it will beat you. I did not fully see until the cancer, how we fight every day against the creeping negativities of the world, how we struggle daily against the slow lapping of cynicism. Dispiritedness and disappointment, these are the real perils of life, not some sudden illness.[1]

The kind of faith Lance Armstrong showed is a deep amalgam of qualities and resources hitherto unknown or untapped, which can lift us to new heights of achievement and energy and which others find irresistible. His words resonate with truth: it is lack of faith which leads us into doubt, disappointment and dispiritedness. When that happens we feel lost, we cannot find a way forward, we do not know how to take the next step.

Faith, therefore, is as fundamental to the survival of the human spirit as food is to the survival of our bodies. With faith, anything is possible; without it, there is nothing. So nurture your own faith, in yourself, in others and in the wonderful possibilities life offers us every day.

One of the most challenging times of my life as a Padre to The Black Watch, that most famous of Scottish Regiments, came about during a six month tour of Belize, when our families back home seemed so very far away. Telephone communication was expensive and rare, and there was always a great surge of eagerness when the mailbag arrived.

It so happened that a situation had arisen within regimental life about which I felt I needed to take an uncompromising and uncomfortable stand – it was far from easy and yet I felt strongly, with Martin Luther King, that 'our lives begin to end when we fail to stand up for those things that matter'. I had placed my reputation at risk, going against what appeared to be the accepted view. As a result I felt very lonely, and worried whether I had done the right thing in the circumstances.

Imagine my delight and relief therefore when, one hot and sultry evening, I saw an envelope among the eagerly anticipated mail on which I recognised the handwriting of my wife Elizabeth. She could not possibly have known of my trials and tribulations at that moment, but her letter assured me not only of how much she loved me but also how fortunate she felt The Black Watch were to have someone of my faith and principles among them.

It was almost as if her belief in me reached out across the oceans to strengthen my faith and so to help me, in the words God spoke to Joshua, to 'Be strong and courageous... for the Lord your God will be with you wherever you go.' (Joshua 1:9)

Faith so very often comes from security, from loving and being loved, from knowing that some things, and people, can forever be trusted and will always be there, and from beliefs which are unshakable.

Allow your faith to blossom and grow. Faith is not a result of what has happened, but a certainty of belief which enables us to cope with whatever we must face.

Faith in our beliefs

In our society today the reaction to those who have deep faith in their religious beliefs is often fear or embarrassment. It is not 'cool' to be religious, to believe in God, to make references to religious faith in television and radio discussions. Those who believe in God are often considered to be anti-reason, anti-science and anti-freedom. However, this attitude overlooks the fact that we live in a culture that relies on its religious foundations and that, far from being unreasonable, Christianity is the foundation stone of much of the achievement of Western civilisation, having made enormous contributions to the development of science, democracy, equal rights and the arts.

Religious faith is still a deeply ingrained part of our national psyche, and countless men and women do have a deep, abiding and growing faith. Those who show evidence of the inner spiritual strength that is faith draw that strength from their beliefs. And those who do not have this faith often express their longing to find it. We have all said, or heard someone say, 'I wish I had your faith.' So how do you find faith?

There can be no better route to faith than by learning from the example of Jesus of Nazareth. He endured terrible suffering, throughout which he was sustained by his own faith in God, his Father. And he was able to inspire faith in those around him, when they were fearful and lost.

Stormy seas and stormy experiences were commonplace in the lives of the first followers of Jesus. Brothers Peter and Andrew and their friends James and John were no strangers to fear – when the winds blew and the sea began to toss and turn they must have feared for their lives. Yet nothing in their prior lives had prepared them for the storm of all storms on the Sea of Galilee, throughout which their leader slept soundly on the bottom of the boat. Eventually they woke him up and said,

150

'Will you not save us?' And so began the miraculous calming of the stormy waters, at the end of which each turned to each the other and said, 'Who is this, that even the winds and the waves obey him?'

No matter what the meteorological or supernatural actualities of that account from the life of Jesus and his earliest disciples might be, there can be no disguising the simple truth that hearts full of fear and panic were calmed, and the stormy tenor of their lives was stilled through the presence of Jesus, with his own momentous faith.

We, in turn, can reach out to Jesus amid the storms and turmoil of our lives. And it is faith which enables us to make that first leap towards him. When we allow his spiritual help and presence to fill our hearts, then we can find faith, and with it serenity, purpose and understanding. We are enriched and enabled to go on with our lives in renewed trust and confidence.

As the letter to the Hebrews reminds us, 'Faith is being sure of what we hope for and certain of what we do not see' (Heb. 11:1). In other words, faith is not an automated religious transaction, but a bold and emphatic renewal of deep inner realities. Paul listed these qualities when he wrote, on another occasion, to friends of his in Galatia. He said, 'The fruit of the Spirit is love, joy, peace, patience, kindness, goodness, faithfulness, gentleness and self-control. Against such things there is no law' (Gal. 5:22–23). And to his friends in Philippi he wrote:

Finally, brothers and sisters, whatever is true, whatever is noble, whatever is right, whatever is pure, whatever is lovely, whatever is admirable – if anything is excellent or praise-worthy – think about such things. Whatever you have learned or received or heard from me, or seen in me – put it into practice. And the God of peace will be with you. (Phil. 4:8–9)

151

The values described in these letters are timeless, and for those who live according to them, faith is both the sum of the parts and the whole which enables each part to exist.

With faith it is possible to believe in miracles. Jesus, many times, performed seemingly miraculous acts, through the power of his faith. And to those who witnessed these miracles, faith was given.

> As Jesus was on his way, the crowds almost crushed him. And a woman was there who had been subject to bleeding for twelve years, but no one could heal her. She came up behind him and touched the edge of his cloak, and immediately her bleeding stopped.
>
> 'Who touched me?' Jesus asked.
>
> When they all denied it, Peter said, 'Master, the people are crowding and pressing against you.'
>
> But Jesus said, 'Someone touched me; I know that power has gone out from me.'
>
> Then the woman, seeing that she could not go unnoticed, came trembling and fell at his feet. In the presence of all the people, she told why she had touched him and how she had been instantly healed. Then he said to her, 'Daughter, your faith has healed you. Go in peace.' (Luke 8:42–48)

For the crowds who witnessed extraordinary moments like these, faith in this young teacher with his wonderful presence and healing gifts must have come willingly and joyfully.

Today we cannot witness Jesus' miracles first-hand. But what we do have are the miracles, small and large, that happen every day in our own lives. The Bible is filled with stories of ordinary people whose faith overcame great obstacles, but so is the world today! All around us there are tales of heroism, determination, courage and perseverance, all born of the absolute faith that 'it can be done'.

There are many wonderful tales of miracles, and of faith born or rediscovered, that come from Lourdes, to the small market town lying in the foothills of the Pyrenees, famous for the apparitions of Our Lady of Lourdes that are reported to have occurred in 1858 to a young miller's daughter, Bernadette Soubirous. The town became a focal point for pilgrims and a site of great healing and I know that, while not everyone can be physically healed, no one leaves Lourdes without gaining in faith. It is a place with an extraordinary peaceful energy which is a balm to the most troubled soul and brings great serenity and joy to all who visit. Lourdes is a centre of faith, and the shared sense of faith to be found there is very powerful.

However, it is not necessary to go to Lourdes to find miracles. The wonderful thing is that we can all find miracles in our lives when we look for them, and every miracle becomes a cornerstone of faith.

Every parent knows that to bring up a child is to witness daily miracles – from birth to first smiles and from first steps to graduations and grandchildren.

Then there is the miracle of friendship. What faith a true friend inspires; there are few things in life more precious. Health and healing are full of wonders too. Every time we recover from an illness, or an injury heals, it is another miracle.

If we pause to look around and appreciate the daily miracles in our lives, then we see faith at every turn, and our own faith cannot help but grow.

When others have faith in us

While faith in our beliefs can become a cornerstone of a life well lived, nothing is more wonderful or more affirming than to find that someone has faith in you. Most people who have achieved success in life can look back and pick out the one or two particular adults who encouraged and believed in them when they were children. Often there has been a special teacher, a relative or a family friend who took the time and trouble to show interest and who had faith in the individual child, even when things might not have looked promising. And as adults too, knowing there is one person who has complete faith in you can give you the self-belief to transform your life.

Jack, a man in his forties, was devastated when he lost his job in the tool factory where he had worked for many years. He dreaded telling his wife, Rose, that they would have no income, and wondered how on earth he would find another job. When he got home his wife saw his drooping shoulders and tired face and asked what was wrong. With a heavy heart Jack told her, but to his astonishment, his wife, instead of looking worried, began to smile. She went into the bedroom and brought back a little box that she kept in a drawer. When she opened it he saw it was full of money. 'There's enough here to keep us for a year,' Rose said. 'Now you can write that novel you've always dreamed of writing. I've always known you could do it, that's why I saved the money.' Jack was astonished by his wife's generosity and faith in him. He began work on his book the following week, and went on to become a highly successful writer.

The faith Jack's wife showed in him inspired him to take a totally new and ultimately fulfilling path in life. Without her support he might have gone on to another dull job and never known what might be possible. It is when we doubt ourselves that the faith of others who believe in us can be the fuel that keeps us going.

I discovered this for myself when I was a young chaplain to both the Parachute Regiment and The Black Watch. I knew that the men of both regiments were facing difficult and test-ing times and would rely on me to help them keep their faith in God, no matter how tough things became. Many times men came to see me, sore at heart, filled with doubts and unsure of their purpose or direction. They missed their families and feared letting down their fellows when up against it. Sometimes it was hard to know how to be there for them, what to say that might restore their strength and purpose. Was I really up to this challenging task? What helped me most, alongside my own faith in Jesus, was knowing that those men had faith in me, and believed I could help them. Their faith in me which they showed by coming to my door in the first place gave me the wisdom and courage I needed to be able to help them.

Faith when times are tough

It is when we are tested that we discover whether or not we have faith in ourselves. And we are all tested during our lives, most of us many times over. We all have to face loss, failure, disappointment, hurt and heartache. At those times we can feel uncertain about how to carry on. The effort of getting out of bed, or putting one foot in front of the other, can seem beyond us. It is then that faith is most needed. Yet if we can find faith, then we can endure, with belief and hope and trust, and know that all will be well and that ultimately our hearts and spirits will be healed.

Sometimes faith is simply a question of gritty determina-tion, as the story of Irwin Rosenberg so beautifully illustrates.

Irwin Rosenberg was a junior officer in the US navy when he was diagnosed with cancer and, according to the standard military procedure of the time, he was discharged. Irwin had loved the navy, and because of this he decided to fight for his health and get his job back. As his illness progressed, there came a point when he was given two weeks to live. But through faith and dogged determination, Irwin survived – and began to recover. Once he had his illness under control, he began to dream of becoming a naval officer again. This, he was told, was impossible. Navy regulations forbade the reinstatement of a person discharged with cancer. 'Give up,' everyone told him. 'It would take an Act of Congress to get you reinstated.' But Irwin didn't give up. If it was going to take an Act of Congress, then he would campaign for that. It took years of waiting, petitioning and battling bureaucracy. But President Truman eventually signed into law a special bill that allowed Irwin Rosenberg to re-enlist in the navy. This he did, and he went on to become a rear admiral in the US Seventh Fleet.

Irwin Rosenberg loved his job so much that he found the determination and faith he needed to overcome his illness and win the job back – faith in himself, in justice and in God. Stories like his, stories of gritty determination, are inspiring and uplifting for everyone who hears them.

Irwin fought for a goal that meant everything to him. But sometimes we need gritty determination alongside our faith simply in order to survive.

In 1987 Terry Waite was kidnapped by an Islamic militia group in Beirut. He had travelled to the troubled city as an envoy for the Church of England, hoping to help secure the release of several Western hostages. Instead he was taken hostage himself and held for almost five years, the first four of them in solitary confinement. He endured fear, loneliness and great hardship, but his faith sustained him, and when he was released he said, 'My sufferings pale into insignificance compared to the suffering of many people in that region.'

Twelve years later he returned to Beirut to visit projects in the Palestinian refugee camps in north Lebanon which were being funded by Y-Care International, the development agency of the YMCA movement, which Waite had helped to found. When he set off for Beirut again, he said, 'Lebanon holds no ghosts or horrors for me.' His faith had not only sustained him, but had allowed him to look back on his experiences without bitterness or hatred.

When we look at stories like those of Terry Waite and the other hostages in Beirut, as well as elsewhere in the world, we begin to understand better the words of St Paul when he said,

> Therefore we do not lose heart. Though outwardly we are wasting away, yet inwardly we are being renewed day by day. For our light and momentary troubles are achieving for us an eternal glory that far outweighs them all. So we fix our eyes not on what is seen, but on what is unseen, since what is seen is temporary, but what is unseen is eternal. (2 Cor. 4:16–18)

How beautifully he puts the simple truth that if we look beyond our present circumstances we will find the courage to survive. And it is faith that allows us to look beyond, to see the 'unseen', that which lies ahead and for which we can strive.

Faith in action

If faith can help us to survive terrible ordeals and inspire others, it can also be our comfort and support when we are setting out on a new endeavour or venture. Such a venture might be the business idea that you have been nursing and nurturing over several months or even years. It may be an adventure you are planning – a mountain climb, a fundraising marathon, a trip across the desert. But it might also be one of the ventures of our everyday lives. Perhaps it is committing to a relationship, bringing a child into the world, hoping to become a good parent, or wanting to be a better and more thoughtful son or daughter.

At times like this it is the voices of others who, in their anxiety for, or jealousy of us may also cast doubt, or whose mocking may seem louder than our own inner voice of faith and trust. Of course we may also have our own inner uncertainties too, an inner voice of doubt and fear which, in the words of Ben Zander, the celebrated conductor of the Boston Philharmonic Orchestra, 'sits on our shoulder as if to say to us: And now you're coming to the difficult bit'.

So how do we rise above the doubters – outward and inward – and find the strength of our own belief in ourselves?

It is then that faith kicks in.

If our faith is strong, we can overcome fear and doubt, reassure those who fear for us, and turn away from those who mock. With faith in ourselves, in our goals, in the power of adventure, we can do extraordinary things.

William Hutchison Murray, forever known as W. H. Murray, was the pioneer of mountaineering in Scotland and in Europe. W. H. Murray was a Scot who longed to share his love of the hills and the mountains with men and women just like himself. During his eighty-three years from 1913 to 1996, Murray took every opportunity, despite the great weight of his mountaineering clothing and the limited kit then available, to try new things. It was W. H. Murray who, along with his friends, opened up many routes that have now become almost commonplace to today's walkers and hill-climbers, and the debt owed to him by modern mountaineers is considerable. W. H. Murray was a brilliant man, a thinker and writer, who wrote this marvellous passage about setting out on a new venture:

Until one is committed, there is hesitancy, the chance to draw back . . . Concerning all acts of initiative (and creation), there is one elementary truth, the ignorance of which kills countless ideas and splendid plans: that the moment one definitely commits oneself, then Providence moves too. All sorts of things occur to help one that would never otherwise have occurred. A whole stream of events issues from the decision, raising in one's favour all manner of unforeseen incidents and meetings and material assistance, which no man could have dreamed would have come his way.

"Whatever you can do, or dream you can do, begin it. Boldness has genius, power and magic in it."

Begin it now.[2]

What a marvellous way of summing up the power of faith. Once you find the faith to set out on your venture, no matter what it is, no matter whether your journey is outwards or inwards once you set off with boldness, you will find your way to your goal, so long as you are prepared to keep going.

A Church of England vicar returned for the first time in a long while to a parish in which he had been very happy for several years. At the end of the special anniversary service which he was conducting, an old lady came up to him and said, 'I always remember one of your sermons and try to practise it daily.' The vicar, delighted to have been not only recognised but also remembered for one of his sermons, eagerly enquired what the sermon had been about. To which the old lady replied, 'I can't actually remember what the subject was, but at the end you said that sometimes we've just got to keep on keeping on! That's what stayed with me.'

Some years back, when I decided to make a long-held dream a reality, I learned for myself that, in addition to boldness born of faith, sometimes there is nothing else to do but 'keep on keeping on'. I wanted to build a centre where people from all walks of life could come to learn the inner greatness of their leadership skills and so go on to fulfil their potential. That was the start of Columba 1400, the charity we named after St Columba, the monk who fled from Ireland to Scotland in AD 563 and founded a monastery on Iona, which became the cradle of Celtic Christianity in Scotland. When we began fund-raising in 1997, it was exactly 1,400 years since the death of this remarkable man.

When almost enough funds had been raised to build our centre, and a perfect site had been found in Staffin on the beautiful island of Skye, work commenced. All seemed to be going well, until I received a call one day to say that the builders had gone into receivership and the half-finished building could not be completed!

It was a heartbreaking moment. Months and months of effort had gone into raising the money and we believed we were nearly there, only to find that the builders' earlier creditors had called in the receivers – they were effectively 'bust'.

For a moment I contemplated giving up. But before I had put the phone down I knew that I could not, and should not. I set about fundraising again, and a few months later the building work was back in progress. When the centre finally opened, three years after we started, I knew it had been worth every back-breaking, heart-wrenching moment of effort.

Since then we have been running leadership academies and retreats for people of all ages and backgrounds, but most especially youngsters from tough realities, who need and deserve an opportunity to realise their own inner greatness, no longer to be the victim or product of their environment, but rather determined to be the people they were created to be. We see young people arrive, cowed and without a shred of self-belief – and see them leave, days later, with their heads high and full of plans for the future. It is a humbling experience.

It was the vision of what might happen in the future that kept me going, and that has kept many thousands of others going, when the going got tough.

Keeping faith

If you are searching for faith, remember that sometimes you will find it where you least expect it. We can pray for faith, but remember also that faith is inspired by our love and care for those around us, as is shown in this story from the anthology *Pathways towards Heaven on Earth* by Sir John Templeton. He tells the story of a Christian monk who earnestly prayed that a vision of Jesus might be revealed to him.

After praying for many hours, the monk heard a voice telling him the vision would occur the next morning at daybreak. Before the first rays of dawn appeared the following morning, the monk was on his knees at the altar.

A fierce storm was brewing but the monk paid it no heed. He watched and prayed and waited for the vision. As the storm broke in great fury, a soft knock came at the door. Interrupted in his devotions, the monk turned away from the altar to open the door. He knew some poor wayfarer was seeking shelter from the raging storm. As he turned towards the door, he caught a glimpse of the vision for which he had prayed.

Torn between his desire to stay and experience the vision – one that he felt would last but for a moment – and his desire to help a brother in distress, the monk quickly decided that duty must come first. Upon opening the door, he gazed into the bright blue eyes of a small child who had apparently lost her way. She was tired, shivering from the cold, and hungry.

The monk gently reached out his hand and led the child

into the warm room. He placed a bowl of milk and some fresh bread before her and did everything he could think of to make her comfortable. Warm, fed and comfortable, the child fell asleep in the chair.

Then, with a heavy heart, the monk turned back towards his altar fearing that the vision had vanished. To his joy and surprise, it was there – clear and bright and shining with radiant glory! As the monk gazed rapturously upon the precious vision for a long time, he heard a voice gently speak: 'If you had not attended to my little one, I could not have stayed.'[3]

The recognition of a link between this life as we know it and the power of God encouraging and guiding us enables the spiritual seeker, despite all the uncertainties, hurts and disappointments of their daily lives, to see their circumstances in an entirely different and fresh way. And this must have been the gripping experience of all those who heard the transformational words of Jesus of Nazareth.

Take, for instance, the parable of the Lost Son, famously known as the Prodigal Son. This is one of Jesus' best-known parables, and has been enormously influential through the centuries.

In the story Jesus describes a father who had two sons. The younger demanded his share of his inheritance and, having been given it, left home and went off to a distant country where he squandered the money on riotous living. Once he was flat broke, he had to take work as a swineherd, working with 'unclean' pigs. Eventually he decided to return home and throw himself on his father's mercy, deciding that even if he was only allowed to be one of his father's servants, it would still be better than feeding pigs. But as the young man returned home, his father spotted him coming and greeted him with open arms, killing a fatted calf in celebration. The older brother, who had been at home all along, resented this favoured treatment and complained at the lack of reward for his own loyalty. But the father said, 'My son, you are always with me, and everything I have is yours. But we had to celebrate and be glad, because this brother of yours was dead and is alive again; he was lost and is found' (Luke 10:31–32).

Those who first heard that story from the lips of Jesus must have felt, like the older brother, that the son should have received a good telling off rather than a celebration party. But the point Jesus was making with this story is profound. At the time he was being criticised by the Pharisees for teaching and eating with sinners, treating them as equals. Jesus told the story to indicate that his loving Father would never lose faith and confidence in us and would always welcome us into his loving arms.

As with the Lost Son, often it is those who wrestle with faith, the apparently least likely characters, whose stories of transcendent spiritual power are the most remarkable and affecting. Dr Albert Schweitzer, that great medical man of faith, described the experience in this way: 'Affirmation of life is the spiritual act by which man ceases to live unreflectively and begins to devote himself to his life with reverence in order to raise it to its true value.'

Ray Charles, the brilliant blind jazz pianist, despite horrendous levels of drug-taking and loose living in his early career, heard the inner voice of faith encouraging him to live a life free from addiction. Clean and dry for the last thirty-five years of his life, his most memorable moment came in the State Legislature in Atlanta, Georgia when the governor sought to apologise to Ray for banning him for life from his home state several years earlier when Ray had refused to play at a 'whites only' concert. When Ray graciously accepted the apology and the lifting of the ban, the governor asked for Ray's permission for one of his most memorable hit songs, 'Georgia On My Mind', to become the state anthem.

Ray was delighted to give his permission.

Ray's wife by his side turned to him and said, 'Wouldn't it be marvellous if your mother could see you now?' Ray replied, 'She's never been away. She's been here all the time.'

Throughout all his trials and tribulations the abiding presence of his mother, who had taught him so much and given him the courage to overcome the fear of his blindness, had never ever left him. It was her deep faith in the resurrection power of Jesus of Nazareth which ultimately brought him through and helped him to make sense of his life.

Ray Charles's mother was the loving, waiting mother whose faith in the goodness and kindness of her child would never leave her.

We all need to keep faith, for faith is the foundation stone of life, the anchor that will see us through the lows and inspire us to reach the highs. Whatever else may come our way, if we have faith – in ourselves, in those we love and in Jesus of Nazareth – then all will be well.

Reflections

Cast your mind back to times when things have been tough. Who was really with you then, who stood by you, listened, encouraged and supported you? Recall with gratitude those people and the qualities they showed that made the difference that enabled you to come through with faith restored.

Consider faith as a bold and emphatic renewal of your deep inner God-given qualities – and whether you are at present 'holding on' or 'setting out', remember the inexhaustible power of the fruits of the Spirit and practise them. Love, joy, peace, patience, kindness, goodness, faithfulness, gentleness and self-control can make such a faith-full difference in your life and in the lives of others.

There will be bad days as well, when the faith-full difference of the fruits of the Spirit appear to be difficult to see, hear or find within you. Seek some time, quietly on your own, a time for forgiveness and for loving redirection, which may lead to amazing new beginnings with family, friends and colleagues.

Begin each day by saying:

Our Father, who art in heaven,
Hallowed be thy name.
Thy kingdom come, thy will be done,
On earth as it is in heaven.
Give us this day our daily bread
And forgive us our trespasses, as we forgive those who trespass
    against us.
And lead us not into temptation, but deliver us from evil.
For thine is kingdom, the power and the glory, for ever.
Amen.

And then, in the faith-full silence, wait, listen, and allow those deep inner qualities to infuse your soul and enthuse your heart so that you might resume your journey all the stronger.

Hope

We have this hope as an anchor
for the soul, firm and secure.

(Heb. 6:19)

Hope is like a flame that cannot and will not be extinguished in the human spirit. We hope, often against great odds, and that hope gives us the energy, the motivation and the determination to carry on.

Many of us have been through tough times. We might have seen a loved one go off the rails, or had cancer or dementia or some other frightening and debilitating illness strike in the family. We may have lost homes, jobs or income due to circumstances beyond our control. At times like this we feel despair and despondency, we do not know where to turn, we lie awake tossing and turning throughout the night, or perhaps sit beside a hospital bed, struggling to continue giving encouragement.

It is at times like these that hope is a wondrous blessing. It helps us to laugh when we thought we would only ever cry again, it gets us back on our feet, it fills us with fresh ideas, new enthusiasm and the will to keep going or try again.

Hope is a glorious thing, as magical as a flower in a patch of thorns or a sunrise after a dark, dark night. When we think we have lost everything, we discover we have not – for there is always hope.

This is why the great English poet Alexander Pope wrote in 1733, in *An Essay on Man*:

Hope springs eternal in the human breast;
Man never Is, but always to be blest:
The soul, uneasy and confin'd from home,
Rests and expatiates in a life to come.

When things are difficult or painful, we need to look ahead to the life to come, believing that good things, good times and happiness will come again. We need to rediscover hopefulness and with it our courage, and we hold onto it like a life raft, knowing that it will see us safely back to the shore.

Vaclav Havel, the Czech poet, playwright, politician and dissident who was imprisoned under the communist regime but eventually went on to become the last president of Czechoslovakia (1989–92) and the first president of the Czech Republic (1993–2003), wrote a wonderful poem about hope.

Either we have hope within us or we don't;
it is a dimension of the soul,
and it's not dependent on some observation of the world.

Hope is an orientation of the spirit, an orientation of the
 heart;
it transcends the world that is immediately experienced,
and is anchored somewhere beyond its horizons.

Hope in this deep and powerful sense,
is not the same as joy that things are going well,
or willingness to invest in enterprises that are
obviously heading for success,
but rather an ability to work for something
because it is good, not just because it
stands a chance to succeed.

> Hope is definitely not the same thing as optimism.
> It is not the conviction that something will turn out well,
> but the certainty that something makes sense,
> regardless of how it turns out.
>
> It is Hope, above all, which gives the strength to live
> and continually try new things.[1]

As Vaclav Havel says so beautifully, hope is not the same as joy or optimism – though it has much in common with both – but rather it is a 'dimension of the soul' which gives us the certainty that something makes sense, and the strength to live and continually try new things.

We all have hope within us, and we can harness that hope to give ourselves strength when we need it most, to share with others when they need it most, and to know, deep in our hearts, what it is that we need to do.

The courageous hopefulness of Jesus

In all of history and literature there has never been a more enduring example of courageous hopefulness than that of Jesus of Nazareth in the Garden of Gethsemane. As has often been argued, Jesus Christ was never more courageous nor more hopeful than on the night before he died. He would have been well aware of his responsibilities and the enormity of the challenge that was facing him. Yet his friends and disciples slept, while he worried and agonised, and were only woken when the authorities came to arrest Jesus and take him away.

The events of that sad night and the days that followed would have been relayed with the extraordinary accuracy of the oral tradition of those days, from person to person over decades, until the time came for the earliest Gospel accounts to be written. Yet not even the agony and sorrow of Jesus' crucifixion on

Good Friday could prevent the joyful resurgence of hope and reunion with his disciples on Easter Day.

Those who followed after Jesus would then, much as we do now, have wondered how he could have endured so much and yet remained so hopeful.

St Paul would undoubtedly have drawn on Jesus' Gethsemane experiences in his own tribulations, so much so that he was later able to write:

> I consider that our present sufferings are not worth comparing with the glory that will be revealed in us . . . The Spirit helps us in our weakness. We do not know what we ought to pray for, but the Spirit himself intercedes for us with wordless groans . . . We know that in all things God works for the good of those who love him, who have been called according to his purpose. (Rom. 8:18, 26, 28)

In his letter to the Christians in Rome, St Paul reminded his readers that they were spiritual heirs and therefore ambassadors of the exemplary selfless love of Jesus of Nazareth, he said:

> For in this hope we were saved. But hope that is seen is no hope at all. Who hopes for what they already have? But if we hope for what we do not yet have, we wait for it patiently. In the same way, the Spirit helps us in our weakness. We do not know what we ought to pray for, but the Spirit himself intercedes for us through wordless groans. (Rom. 8:24–26)

Writing in such a deeply personal and sensitive manner, St Paul was able to convey to his readers that he understood them and knew what they were going through. Again and again he emphasised the quality of hope, being ready always to take the long-term view, for, 'We know that in all things God works for the good of those who love him, who have been called according to his purpose' (Rom. 8:28).

St Paul even went so far as to write:

Who shall separate us from the love of Christ? Shall trouble or hardship or persecution or famine or nakedness or danger or sword? . . . No, in all these things we are more than conquerors through him who loved us. For I am convinced that neither death nor life, neither angels nor demons, neither the present nor the future, nor any powers, neither height nor depth, nor anything else in all creation, will be able to separate us from the love of God that is in Christ Jesus our Lord. (Rom. 8:35, 37–39)

I have often wondered if St Paul ever knew how encouraging his words would prove not just for those to whom he wrote, but also for the countless readers since who have been inspired by him not to lose hope. In the writing of his letters St Paul was taking a considerable personal risk but also giving lively evidence of the faith and hope that was in him, faith which would endure and abide.

Later on in his life St Paul sent not one, but two letters of hopeful exhortation and encouragement to the young man Timothy, seeking to remind Timothy that 'God did not give us a spirit of timidity, but a spirit of power, of love and of self-discipline' (2 Tim. 1:7).

Indeed, this source of power, love and self-discipline can be for each one of us an inner strength waiting to be recognised and released.

Cultivate a hopeful heart

Although we all have the seeds of hopefulness in us, there is much that we can do to nurture those seeds into something far bigger and stronger that can sustain us when we most need it.

Sometimes when our dreams appear to be shattered we can become tempted to lose hope, to wonder what life is all about. In our ready-made, fast-food, consumerist society we can feel worthless, as if our lives will make no difference whatsoever to the lives of our fellow human beings. Yet all around us there are astonishing stories of great hope and encouragement which help us to cultivate hope in our own hearts.

W. F. Deedes, in his book *Brief Lives*, told the story of how an illegitimate boy from Lossiemouth in the north of Scotland, the son of a scullery maid, rose to become the first Labour prime minister of Britain in 1924. His name was Ramsay MacDonald. After barely a year in office, his party lost power. MacDonald was exhausted after the trials and tribulations of political life and what he wrote after that defeat tells us a great deal about him and his Highland roots.

> Sometimes one must flee from familiar things and faces and voices, from the daily round and the common task, because one's mind becomes a bit of green grass too much trod upon. It has to be protected and nursed, and it has to be let alone. Then, give me the hill road, the bleating of the sheep, the clouds, the sun and the rain, the graves of dead races, the thatched roofs of living ones, a pipe and a fire when the day is closing, and a clean bed to lie upon until the sun calls in the morning. If friends fail, the hill road never does.

Ramsay MacDonald's 'hill road' enabled him to recover and ultimately to become prime minister of Great Britain once again, this time for six years, through the Great Depression of the 1930s, at the head of a coalition government. Without doubt it was because of his 'hill road', the familiar place to which he could return to find peace and healing, that his sense of hopefulness again saw the light of day and so went on to encourage others once more.

We all need to find our own 'hill road' – a place of peace and renewal, calm and clarity, in which we can recover our energy and our hope.

Jesus of Nazareth certainly had several places where he could be alone and commune, without interruption, with the powerful healing and encouraging presence of his ever-loving Father. From his earliest days when Jesus reassured his parents not to be worried about him because he needed to spend time in the temple and 'be about his Father's business', he must have practised the art of silence, meditation and prayer and those times undoubtedly strengthened his faith and his hope for what was to lie ahead.

Jesus knew the Hebrew Scriptures well and throughout his trials and temptations he would have drawn great comfort from them. Knowing the prophecies of Isaiah by heart, he would have been able to recite inwardly and regularly:

> Do you not know?
> Have you not heard?
> The Lord is the everlasting God,
> the Creator of the ends of the earth.
> He will not grow tired or weary,
> and his understanding no one can fathom.
> He gives strength to the weary
> and increases the power of the weak.
> Even youths grow tired and weary,
> and young men stumble and fall;
> but those who hope in the Lord
> will renew their strength.
> They will soar on wings like eagles;
> they will run and not grow weary,
> they will walk and not be faint.
> (Isa. 40:28–31)

Those who hope in the Lord will renew their strength. We can only imagine the despondency and broken-heartedness of the disciples in witnessing their friend and leader humiliated, crucified and finally laid to rest in a tomb. They must surely have felt grief-stricken as they rested, after his death, on the Sabbath day, according to the Jewish custom.

The next morning two of them decided to make their way to a village called Emmaus, some seven miles from Jerusalem, and on the journey they were discussing all the things that had happened.

While they were talking, Jesus himself came near and accompanied them, but they did not recognise him. As with heavy hearts they discussed what had happened and how Jesus had been crucified and died, they said to him, 'You see, we had hoped that he was the one to redeem Israel.' As they neared Emmaus, Jesus walked ahead as if to go on, but they persuaded him to stay and have supper with them. When Jesus was at the table with them he took bread, blessed and broke it, and gave it to them, at which their eyes were opened and they recognised him – and as they did so their hope was renewed.

'Were not our hearts burning within us while he was talking to us on the road?' This oft-repeated quote from the New Testament encapsulates in one sentence so many of our experiences of 'hopelessness' which can yet become unexpected 'hopefulness'. It reminds us that even when we feel hope is absent, it will return, and we can trust in that.

To cultivate a hopeful heart, then, is to remember that hope will always be renewed and that there must always be a place for hope in the human spirit.

William Duff is a young man whose spirit has never faltered, and who, even when he faced great difficulties, never let go of hope. I met William a few years ago at his school prize giving. For years he had been ill with ME and Gilbert's Syndrome.

His illness was so severe that he was unable to go to school. Confined to a wheelchair and at times completely bedridden, he suffered severe muscle wastage, along with a catalogue of other symptoms. He was educated by a tutor who came once a week for two hours, and apart from that had to teach himself.

William dreamed of going to university to study accountancy, but as the illness continued to debilitate him, his dream seemed impossible. Still he persevered, studying for and passing all the exams he needed.

With intensive physiotherapy William was eventually able to go from a wheelchair to a zimmer frame, and then to crutches. To his delight, and that of his family, he won a place at Glasgow Caledonian University to study accountancy. William threw himself into university life during his first year, and managed to get work in the summer holidays with an accountancy firm in his home town of Tain. The firm's bosses were so impressed with him that an offer of two weeks' unpaid work became six weeks' paid work and he was invited back the following summer, by which time he was able to walk without his crutches. By his third year at university William had won an internship for the summer with PricewaterhouseCoopers, one of the big four accountancy firms in Britain.

William refused to give up on his dream, despite his illness. He worked phenomenally hard and even when he was bedridden, he continued to hope that he would make it. His success is well deserved, and gives hope to others in similar circumstances.

Finish the race

Vaclav Havel's words, that hope is 'a dimension of the soul', creates an image of hope as something to be cherished, guarded and trained – rather in the manner of an Olympic athlete, whose oath from those earliest Olympian days in Athens has read, 'I have prepared. I have followed the rules. I will not quit.' This is no spurious armchair concept, nor is it akin to a swift dash outside to see which way the wind is blowing. No, such a definition of hope, as a dimension of the soul, is what keeps us running when it might appear to some that the race is finished, or even that the spectators have left the stadium. And, as this wonderful story shows, sometimes the race is not over, and the spectators are hanging on:

Over an hour after the winner had crossed the line in the marathon of the 1968 Olympics in Mexico City, one man was still running. Suddenly a small wiry man limped slowly into the stadium. He stopped every couple of steps because of the pain in his right leg. A hastily prepared bandage covered his right knee. His name? John Stephen Akhwari of Tanzania.

He had fallen during the race, cutting his knee and dislocating the joint. He was bleeding and every step sent a wave of pain throughout his exhausted body. He tried to run, but the pain was too great. He resorted to a slow walk interspaced with short painful attempts at running.

The crowd, which had been beginning to drift away, decided to stay and was moved by the courage of that seventy-fourth competitor. The silence was broken by heartfelt clapping, egging Akhwari on to finish the race. And with his every step, the cheering grew louder, until the stadium was roaring with admiration for this man who would not give up. As he crossed the finish line, the multitudes erupted, cheering as if he had won the gold medal.

Reporters asked him why he opted to endure the excruciating pain and why he had not retired once there was no chance of him winning. He was surprised by the question, pondered for a moment, then said, 'I don't think you understand. My country did not send me to Mexico City to start the race. They sent me to finish the race.'

This story of true bravery and endurance is a reminder of the power of unquenchable hope, and the honour that belongs to those who 'finish the race' and do what must be done, no matter what it costs. History is full of stories of those whose hope has triumphed over exhaustion, failure, setbacks and disappointments.

The great American writer William Faulkner endured many a rejection in his desire to become a novelist. At those times he experienced the hopelessness of despair. Would the personal sacrifice of time and energy he was making ever be worthwhile? Was he being fair to those who relied on him and who loved him? Yet William Faulkner gradually began to see that 'hopelessness' can be transformed into 'hopefulness', so that when he ultimately received the greatest accolade of his life, the Nobel Prize for Literature in 1949, he said in his acceptance speech, 'I believe that man will not merely endure: he will prevail. He is immortal, not because he alone among creatures has an inexhaustible voice, but because he has a soul, a spirit capable of compassion and sacrifice and endurance.'

Frère Roger of the Taizé Community wrote these wonderfully hopeful words, celebrating man's compassion and endurance, shortly before his death.

Seeking reconciliation and peace involves a struggle within oneself. It does not mean taking the line of least resistance. Nothing lasting is created when things are too easy. The spirit of communion is not gullible. It causes the heart to become more encompassing; it is profound kindness; it does not listen to suspicions.

To be bearers of communion, will each of us walk forward in our lives of trust and of a constantly renewed kind-heartedness?

On this road there will be failures at times. Then we need to remember that the source of peace and communion is in God. Instead of becoming discouraged, we shall call down His Holy Spirit upon our weaknesses. And, our whole life long, the Holy Spirit will enable us to set out again and again, going from one beginning to another towards a future of peace.[2]

We need look no further than great figures of recent history to see hopefulness in action. The spirit of Britain's great wartime leader Sir Winston Churchill has often been quoted and when others were scared and worried he seemed to find his greatest inner resources. Indeed, without his courage the history of the United Kingdom and indeed of the civilised world might have been very different. In October 1941, in the darkest days of the Second World War, Winston Churchill was asked to visit Harrow, his old school, and to address the pupils. There he memorably said, 'I have only seven words for you. Never, never ever, never ever, give in.'

Most of us know what it is to set out again and again, but if we can find the courage to pick ourselves back up after every knock or doubt and not give in, then we can follow hope, as if it were a light shining ahead of us to clear our path.

Three young Americans, full of hope and resilience, each had their own business idea. One had a creative idea about the processing of cheese, and began his business with a horse and cart selling his cheese door to door. Another rode his bicycle door to door selling hand-painted greeting cards. The third opened a 'Golden Rule Store' and everyone who came to his store was treated in accord with the maxim, as the young businessman himself would wish to have been treated. These three young men had one thing in common – they started out with nothing and became world famous. But Mr Kraft, Mr Hall and Mr Penney had something far more fundamental in common than their ultimate success – they literally took their faith and hope with them to work. No one working for Kraft, Hall and Penney could have been unaware that their founders looked to their faith and hope in God when making business decisions. And the families, friends and business associates of Messrs Kraft, Hall and Penney were never allowed to forget that their business enterprises were to be 'ministries of service' to others.

Although they were ultimately hugely successful, each of these three men went through many trials and tribulations on the way, and they needed deep inner resources of courage and tenacity, hope and perseverance in order to 'finish the race' they had begun.

Another inspiring example of a man who 'finished the race' is Nelson Mandela. When he was tried and sent to prison for life in 1963, for 'crimes' committed as one of the leaders of the anti-apartheid movement, he told the court, 'I'll be back.' It was not until twenty-seven years later – eighteen of them spent on Robben Island and a total of nine in solitary confinement – that he was freed from prison and did indeed come back to continue what he had begun, completing a long journey to help bring freedom, equality and peace to the people of South Africa.

On the first Reconciliation Day in South Africa on 16 December 1995, Nelson Mandela, by then president, said:

> We have, in real life, declared our shared allegiance to justice, non-racialism and democracy; our yearning for a peaceful and harmonious nation of equals.
>
> The rainbow has come to be the symbol of our nation. We are turning the variety of our languages and cultures, once used to divide us, into a source of strength and richness. But we do know that healing the wounds of the past and freeing ourselves of its burden will be a long and demanding task. This

day of reconciliation celebrates the progress we have made; it reaffirms our commitment; and it measures the challenges.

We must use our collective strengths to carry on building the nation and improving its quality of life.

Thus we shall free ourselves from the burden of yesteryear; not to return there; but to move forward with the confidence of free men and women, committed to attain the best for ourselves and future generations.

What better message of hope to convey to the peoples of South Africa and to the world? And what better symbol of hope than the rainbow? For some years before he was freed, South Africa had the potential to become one of the bloodiest places on earth. Nelson Mandela never lost his personal sense of hope, despite all those years when he must have wondered if he would ever be free, and he brought hope to many millions of others and helped to transform his nation from one of bloodshed and strife to one in which peoples shared a common future in which all believed.

Give hope to others

The time when we are tempted to give up or think that we have failed very often turns out to immediately precede the point when life will begin to make sense or take shape – as long as we do not lose hope. Indeed it is often said that 'the sun is at its brightest just before dawn.' And as we are able to make sense of our own lives, and through our hope and faith to build our serenity and wisdom, so we will find ourselves able to support and encourage others.

Several years ago I remember feeling that I had to take a public stand on an issue about which I felt strongly conscience driven. As a result the leader writers of the national press took a pop at me, from their usual comfortable distance. However much those who loved and supported me reminded me that 'today's newspapers are tomorrow's fish and chip papers', the comments inevitably hurt. Imagine my delighted surprise, therefore, when I received, during this uneasy and difficult time, a signed Bible from two friends with the inscription 'Philippians 4 verses 4 to 9 is our gift to you'.

I will never forget how helpful and comforting it was to read those verses:

> Rejoice in the Lord always; again I will say, Rejoice. Let your gentleness be known to everyone. The Lord is near. Do not worry about anything, but in everything by prayer and supplication with thanksgiving let your requests be made known to God. And the peace of God, which surpasses all understanding, will guard your hearts and your minds in Christ Jesus. (NRSV)

The passage concludes with these memorable and hopeful words for all who are prepared to take a stand for something which they know in their heart of hearts to be true, right and of value:

> Finally, beloved, whatever is true, whatever is honourable, whatever is just, whatever is pure, whatever is pleasing, whatever is commendable, if there is any excellence and if there is anything worthy of praise, think about these things. (Phil. 4:8)

That generous gift helped me greatly and, along with the support of those around me, gave me the strength of spirit to stick to what I believed to be right.

The opportunity to encourage someone who has temporarily faltered, or lost heart, or is unsure of how to move forward, is a wonderful thing – a gift you receive, through giving of yourself. Look around you, and see who there is in your life who needs a word of encouragement, or some practical or moral support. Do what you can to help those who need hope and as they recover and begin to blossom, you will feel a powerful sense of peace, love and completion.

Two men, both seriously ill, occupied the same hospital room. One man was allowed to sit up in his bed for an hour each afternoon to help drain the fluid from his lungs. His bed was next to the room's only window. The other man had to spend all his time flat on his back. The men talked for hours on end. They spoke of their wives and families, their homes, their jobs, their involvement in the military service and where they had been on holiday. And every afternoon when the man in the bed by the window could sit up, he would pass the time by describing to his roommate all the things he could see outside the window.

The man in the other bed began to live for those one-hour periods when his world would be broadened and enlivened by all the activity and colour of the world outside. The window overlooked a park with a lovely lake. Ducks and swans played on the water, while children sailed their model boats. Young lovers walked arm in arm amid flowers of every colour of the rainbow. Grand old trees graced the landscape, and a fine view of the city skyline could be seen in the distance.

As the man by the window described all this in exquisite detail, the man on the other side of the room would close his eyes and imagine the picturesque scene, and gradually he began to feel better and to heal.

Days and weeks passed. One morning, the nurse arrived to find that the man by the window had died peacefully in his sleep. As soon as it seemed appropriate, the other man asked if he could be moved next to the window. The nurse was happy to make the switch, and after making sure he was comfortable, she left him alone. Slowly, he propped himself up on one elbow to take his first look at the world outside. Finally, he would have the joy of seeing it for himself. He turned to look out of the window. It faced a blank wall. All the wonderful scenes his roommate had described had been created in his mind. With a tender heart, the man realised what great generosity his friend had shown, in order to give him encouragement and hope.

Mahatma Gandhi, the great political and spiritual leader of India during the independence movement, once said, 'Be the change that you want to see in the world.' To give hope, be hopeful. Even when there seem to be few reasons to hope, you can find hope, and share it, and so enrich others.

Sometimes all it takes to rekindle hope is a simple word of encouragement.

When the great composer Rachmaninoff was at the peak of his success, loved by audiences and critics alike, he wrote a symphony which turned out to be a complete disaster. It must have come as a complete shock to him for he became disconsolate, discouraged and full of self-pity. He moped around to such an extent that even his close friends and family could not help him and his musical career seemed to have come to an untimely end.

In desperation, one of his cousins took him to see Dr Nicholas Dahl who, having listened to him, began to spend time with him repeating such memorable phrases as, *'great things lie dormant within you, waiting to be given to the world'*, *'you will start to compose a concerto: you will work with the greatest of ease: the composition will be of excellent quality'*. Such phrases became the turning point. Rachmaninoff took this hopeful encouragement to heart and began to repeat the phrase, *'great things lie dormant in you, waiting to be given to the world,'* over and over again to himself until he felt a renewed sense of hope and purpose.

He felt his musical confidence and talent return in the manner in which atrophied muscles can be built up and strengthened after an injury. Several months later he felt able to compose a full Concerto which he dedicated to Doctor Nikolai Dahl and which became the famous Concerto No2 in C Minor. When the concerto was first performed, in Nobility Hall in Moscow, the audience gave Rachmanioff an uplifting, prolonged and noisy standing ovation.

How important it was for the great composer, in his despair, to step back a bit, to rekindle his faith and rediscover the hope that was lying dormant in his soul. As St Paul was to the young Timothy, so Doctor Dahl was to the young Rachmaninoff.

Not all of us, however, can produce symphonies. Sometimes we are so busy focusing on a faraway goal that we forget to see what is under our nose. In another lovely story, a teacher at the end of his career needed to be reminded of all he had achieved, and all the hope he had given to those in his care over the years.

The film *Mr Holland's Opus* tells the story of a high school music teacher who dreamed of writing a world-class symphony and, through his music, becoming famous and wealthy. When he took a teaching job he planned to use his spare time to compose, but somehow teaching took up all his time and his composing had to take a back seat. When, after a long career, the time came for him to retire, Mr Holland felt dejected and a failure. What, after all, had his life been all about?

On his final day, as he prepared to leave the school buildings for the last time, his wife walked him over to the school gymnasium and into a surprise party which had been organised in his honour by hundreds of his former students. The leading organiser was a woman who, as a schoolgirl, had lacked confidence and considered herself to be a failure. Through Mr Holland's encouragement she had found value in herself and gone on to become governor of her home state.

In her speech on behalf of the entire gathering she said, 'We are your Symphony, Mr Holland. We are the melodies and notes of your Opus. We are the music of your life.'

This wonderful affirmation of a life well lived and filled with generosity is a poignant reminder of the good work so many people do, without plaudits or praise, prizes or platforms.

There are times, however, when words of hope or encouragement are simply not enough. Well-meaning phrases can appear hollow to someone in deep distress, who might think, 'How could they possibly know what I'm going through? They wouldn't be able to speak like that if they really knew how hopeless I feel.' Sometimes in our pain and despair we close down to those who love us and even to the possibility of spiritual help, support or guidance. But lonely as we may feel, it is undoubtedly then that God is closest to us, as the unknown author wrote so beautifully:

> One night I dreamed a dream.
> I was walking along the beach with the Lord.
> Many scenes from my life flashed across the sky.
> In each scene I noticed footprints in the sand.
> Sometimes there were two sets of footprints,
> other times there was only one.
>
> This bothered me because I noticed
> that during the low periods of my life,
> when I was suffering from anguish, sorrow or defeat,
> I could see only one set of footprints.

So I said to the Lord,
'You promised me, Lord,
that if I followed you,
you would walk with me always.
But I have noticed that during
the most trying periods of my life
there has been only one set of footprints in the sand.
Why, when I needed you most,
have you not been there for me?'

The Lord replied,
'The times when you have seen
only one set of footprints, my child,
is when I carried you.'[3]

Even when there seem to be few reasons to hope and the world appears to be a dark place, there is hope, help and love at hand. In his darkest hour, Jesus knew that his Father was there for him, as Jesus is there for us when we need him most.

In that joyful knowledge, hope can flourish and we find the strength, resilience and courage to persevere.

It is in our darkest moments that the power of prayer becomes a wonderful resource. When we pray, we realise that we are not alone, and the sense that there is a higher power there to share the burden is enormously comforting.

And so, as we build our faith and restore our hope, we can focus on the quality that is more powerful even than these two – love.

Reflections

Recall a story in which hope triumphed over despair. Retell that story when the opportunity presents itself – and remember that you too have your hope-full stories. Treasure them, recall them, retell them: in this way you are becoming a hope-full person and passing on a real-life banner of hope.

Find your 'hill road', a simple quiet place where your hope-full qualities can be cherished and restored. Remember that when you feel at your most hopeless, it is then that God is carrying you and so restoring you for the next hope-full stage of your journey.

Think of the difference you might be able to make to the next person you meet today and tomorrow and in the days after. Offer support, encouragement and hope to those who need it.

Remember that our lives are like clay in the potter's hand and that every day we are being refined through life's experiences to become fully human and fully alive as God created us to be. Such an awareness will be the well-spring of our hope.

Pray this prayer of the Unknown Confederate Soldier:

I asked God for strength, that I might achieve,
I was made weak, that I might learn humbly to obey.
I asked God for health, that I might do greater things,
I was given infirmity, that I might do better things.
I asked for riches, that I might be happy,
I was given poverty, that I might be wise.
I asked for power, that I might have the praise of men,
I was given weakness, that I might feel the need of God.
I asked for all things, that I might enjoy life,
I was given life, that I might enjoy all things.
I got nothing that I asked for, but everything I had hoped for.
Almost despite myself, my unspoken prayers were answered.
I am among men, most richly blessed.

Love

In his Gospel, in a dazzling intuition,
St John expresses who God is in three words:
'God is Love.'
If we can grasp only those three words,
we shall go far, very far.[1]

(Frère Roger, Taizé)

Love is all around us – in songs, stories, plays, on the radio, on the television, in films and in art. In the Western world we focus most often on romantic love, the love between a man and a woman, usually young, good looking and either destined to live 'happily ever after', or irrevocably doomed. We love extremes, we love to celebrate romance, or cry over it. But in our excitement over romantic love, we can forget that love is so much more than this.

When we look around the world, and look at history, we find many different interpretations and versions of love. The ancient Greeks, for instance, defined love in three ways. First of all there was *philia*, which we now interpret in terms of philanthropy, love and generosity shown towards our fellow human beings, based on friendship. Second, there was *eros*, the sensual and erotic aspects of love, dealing with desire. Third, there was *agape*, love which sustains and maintains and denotes a general sense of contentment and good feeling.

The early Celtic Christian peoples also defined love in three different ways, which are just as contemporary and relevant for us now. Love was all about warmth: first, warmth of welcome; second, warmth of hospitality; and third, the warmth of being on a shared journey – values that we used as the basis of Columba 1400 when we began it and which sustain us as we continue our work.

In so many societies, past and present, romantic love has been rightly seen as such a small aspect of love as a whole. Love was, and is, so much greater, encompassing the warmth, humanity, fellow feeling, joy and generosity that makes us human. Love, which is essentially goodwill and fellow feeling for the rest of humanity, is the foundation stone of all that truly matters and all that is good in the world.

Frère Roger of the Taizé Community in France asked:

What does it mean to love?

Could it be to share the suffering of the most ill-treated? Yes, that's it. Could it mean having infinite kind-heartedness and forgetting oneself for others, selflessly? Yes, certainly. What does it mean to love? Loving means forgiving, living as people who are reconciled. And reconciliation always brings a springtime to the soul.[2]

It is this joyful image, a 'springtime to the soul', which we all long to discover and experience. Spring is all about awakening, blossoming and growing, and this is what happens in our souls when we experience love – for ourselves, for those close to us, and for all mankind.

Of course, to love is to risk hurt and disappointment, loss and fear, and so there are those who close themselves off to love, not daring to take the risk. This is sad, because loving is a risk worth taking. Yes, sometimes love means loss; it may mean having to give up the person you love; certainly love often involves letting go. But those who love fully and deeply are the richer for it, no matter what the outcome.

When you become fully and authentically loving towards yourself and others, you begin to realise that your life is not counted by the years lived, but by love offered and experiences shared. So open yourself to love, let your heart be filled with love, and delight in the gifts that loving and being loved can bring.

Build on rock

Before you can love others, you must love yourself. And by love, here, I mean *accept*. When you can say, 'I like myself, I'm fine, I do my best, I'm good enough,' and feel it in your heart, then you have achieved something marvellous. So many people, via their upbringing or childhood influences, feel that they are not good enough and spend a great deal of time criticising themselves. In humanistic therapy they refer to the 'top dog' – the part of oneself that judges, criticises, condemns, badgers, that looks at what you did not do today, not at what you did do, and generally gives you a hard time. The 'underdog' part of you whimpers and agrees that you really are a bad person, and feels guilty and wretched. In therapy people are encouraged to strengthen the underdog and stand up to the top dog by saying, 'Actually I'm fine, I did well today, I'm good enough.'

This kind of positive affirmation is simple and effective. Telling yourself, out loud if possible, that you like and approve of yourself, does work. Do it often, many times a day, because that way the message hits home and the top dog has less space to snap and snarl at you.

Another potential route to self-acceptance and a greater sense of love is to encourage gratitude. When we are thankful for all that we have, when we appreciate the small blessings and joys in our lives, then our hearts open and fill with love. It is impossible to feel grateful without feeling loving. So practise gratitude, every day. An attitude of gratitude is an attitude of happiness which can, and does bring opportunities. Give thanks, out loud, in a journal, in prayers, or just with hugs and smiles, for all that you have and are.

Self-acceptance is not about vanity or self-obsession. It is about being at peace with yourself, being comfortable in your own skin, freeing your energy for more constructive and important things than snapping at your own heels.

Perhaps that is what Jesus had in mind when he told the story of the contrasting fortunes of the two men who built their houses, one upon rock and one upon sand. If, like the second builder, your love is built on the shifting sands of self-doubt and dislike, then it will be difficult to hold onto anything or anyone, let alone nurture your own soul. If, however, your love is built on the firmer ground of self-acceptance, then you will have the best foundation of all for your life and for your future and for all those around you.

When we have a right self-love, we are able to love others and to give generously of ourselves and our love. And we are able to receive love. Self-dislike and doubt shut the door to love, even when it is offered to us. If we do not feel lovable, then how can we feel loved? Many people push love away when it is given to them, believing that they cannot possibly be loved, because they are so unlovable.

The second most important commandment, 'Love your neighbour as yourself' (Mark 12:31), does not mean loving our neighbours *instead* of ourselves. It means loving our neighbours – that is, others – as we would like to be loved ourselves. In other words, first spend time getting to know and accept yourself, so that you can demonstrate love and understanding towards others.

To create a rock-like foundation of love in our lives we must learn to love ourselves, in order to give and receive love with others. St Irenaeus, the second-century Christian bishop and writer, said, 'The Glory of God is a human being fully alive.' This wonderful statement is as true today as it was almost two thousand years ago. To be fully alive is to feel love, to the depth of your being. When we love, we are awake, alert, joyful and grateful for being alive.

Jesus of Nazareth said, 'I have come that they may have life, and have it to the full' (John 10:10). He brought love, in all its richness and joyfulness. Jesus loved, deeply and fully, all those who came in contact with him, and through that gift of love he brought life in all its fullness.

When you are able to accept yourself, you will find you are also able to let go of habits that are holding you back. Addictions of all kinds are a way of distancing ourselves from feelings which are uncomfortable or difficult to accept. But to feel is to be alive, and when we accept ourselves we accept our feelings, whatever they may be. A feeling is not an action. To feel angry or hurt is not to hurt or damage others in itself. We can accept our 'negative' feelings without judging ourselves and without acting on those feelings. Self-acceptance, which is self-love, allows us to see our feelings without fearing them, and without the need to be cruel, cutting, violent or unkind to others.

Think of yourself as a newborn, with all the potential of a new young life. We are all born with such potential for purity and achievement, and we should strive to hold on to that potential, no matter what may have happened in our lives.

Our new and rock-solid foundations will be based on love, when we realise that each and every one of us is precious in God's sight and that we have been made, in the words of Souza, to dance, love, sing and live.

> Dance as though no one is watching you
> Love as though you have never been hurt
> Sing as though no one can hear you
> Live as though heaven is on earth.[3]

Being loved

When you are with someone whom you love and who loves you unconditionally, you feel you can do anything and cope with anything. There is no more wonderful feeling in the world than being loved, and for a small child it creates a sense of safety in the world that nothing else can replicate.

I remember as a young boy cycling home one evening after rugby practice. I was in a hurry as I was late, and pedalled furiously – so hard that I crashed headlong into Mr Wilkinson, the groundsman at the rugby club, who was on his way to catch his bus. Luckily he was not badly hurt, but I flew off my bike and hit the gravel. I limped home with bleeding knees and grazed elbows, feeling very sorry for myself.

When I arrived home my mother said nothing, she simply lifted me in her arms and carried me upstairs for the treat of all treats, a warm soapy bath in my parents' bathroom. To this day I can see the love and compassion in her eyes, and feel her tender fingers picking out the grit from my knees and face and bandaging my elbows.

Although it took me some time to recover outwardly, inwardly I was sound and secure because I knew that no matter what had happened or what might happen, my mother loved me.

If we are lucky enough to have the love of a parent, then we have a head start in life. And if we are then able to find a loving partner who accepts us no matter what, we are doubly blessed.

When Duncan got ready for work one Friday morning, he announced to his wife that he had finally decided to ask his boss for a salary raise. All day Duncan felt nervous and apprehensive as he thought about the coming showdown. What if his boss refused to grant his request? Duncan had worked so hard in the last two years at the advertising agency. He thought he deserved a wage increase. Late in the afternoon he finally mustered up the courage to approach his boss, who, to his delight and surprise, agreed to give Duncan a raise.

Duncan arrived home that evening – breaking all speed limits – to a beautiful table set with their best china, and candles lit. His wife Tina had prepared his favourite food. Someone from the office must have tipped her off!

Next to his plate Duncan found a beautiful note from his wife. It read: 'Congratulations, my love! I knew you'd get the raise! I prepared this dinner to show just how much I love you. I am so proud of your accomplishments!' He read it and stopped to reflect on how sensitive and caring Tina was.

After dinner, Duncan was on his way to the kitchen to get dessert when he noticed that a second card had slipped out of Tina's pocket onto the floor. He bent forward to retrieve it and read: 'Don't worry about not getting the raise! You deserve it anyway! You are a wonderful provider and I prepared this dinner to show you just how much I love you even though you did not get the increase.'

Suddenly tears filled Duncan's eyes. Tina's love and support was not conditional on his success at work.

The fear of rejection is often softened when we know that someone loves us regardless of our success or failure. In fact, knowing that we are loved can give us the courage to try and try again and to undergo almost any setback or rejection.

Think about those who love you – friends, partner, family, children – and allow yourself, for a moment, to feel their love in your heart and in your soul. Being loved is an honour and a joy. To know that you are loved simply for being you is the greatest gift of all.

Those early Celtic Christian values, of warmth of welcome and hospitality and of the sense of being on a shared journey, underpin the work of Columba 1400. Young people of all ages and stages, and most particularly those from tough realities, find real warmth in the love which is extended to each and every one of them.

Some graduates from the Columba 1400 Leadership Programmes feel for the very first time something burning in their hearts, a feeling which they have never felt or recognised before. Like a flower coming into bloom, there is a recognition that, as one person commented, 'Other people not only know me, but they also like me and trust me and say they love me!' Another said, 'Life can begin again, for now I feel part of something really worthwhile.'

There is also a sense of community and well-being in the knowledge that others feel similarly. As one young graduate said recently, 'After all I have been through, here at last is a group of people, a loving caring community, who trust and respect me and whom I can trust and respect.'

Graduation ceremonies at Columba 1400 often reflect the incredulity we can all feel when something we thought we had lost or would never discover appears in our hearts.

When you know that you are loved, then you can realise that you are a truly lovable person. The early Celtic Christians had a phrase for this sense of feeling loved and lovable: *Anam Cara*. Loosely translated, this means 'dear soul', and it is now often translated as 'soul mate'. The *Anam Cara* described a dear soul who knew you and loved you almost better than you knew or loved yourself; someone to whom you could go at any time and never feel a nuisance, someone who could read your eyes and know in a moment how you were feeling. Such an *Anam Cara* is present in the words of the prophet Isaiah:

> I have summoned you by name; you are mine.
> When you pass through the waters,
> I will be with you;

and when you pass through the rivers,
they will not sweep over you.
When you walk through the fire,
you will not be burned;
the flames will not set you ablaze.
. . . you are precious and honoured in my sight
. . . I love you.
(Isa. 43:1–4)

In *Billy Elliot*, the award-winning film and stage production, Billy's *Anam Cara* was his dancing teacher Mrs Wilkinson, who stood in the gap with him. Billy was the son of a miner whose mother had died, and he learned to dance despite mockery from most of the boys and men around him. Mrs Wilkinson believed in him, encouraged him and eventually persuade him to audition for the Royal School of Ballet.

During the audition an examiner asked Billy what it felt like when he was dancing. Billy replied that he couldn't really explain it because he hadn't got the words. It was a feeling that he couldn't control, like forgetting and losing who you are but at the same time feeling whole. Looking quizzically at the examiners he said that it was like hearing your first ever music playing in your ear and listening and listening and then disappearing until something deep inside was felt, like a fire within, something bursting, impossible to hide. Very quietly he added that it felt as if he was flying, like a bird, like electricity sparking inside him and he was free.

When we know that we are loving, loved and lovable, there rises in our spirit an electricity that enables us, like Billy Elliot, to feel free – free from our past, released to become who we were meant to be.

The famous nineteenth-century professor of science and religion, Henry Drummond, described those feelings of electricity in his best-selling book *The Greatest Thing in the*

World: 'You will find as you look back on your life that the moments that stand out, the moments when you have really lived, are the moments when you have done things in a spirit of love.'

Loving others

Mitch Albom in *Tuesdays with Morrie* wrote, 'One day spent with someone you love can change everything.' When we love others, we become generous, we are willing to make sacrifices, we shift mountains and we can do the impossible.

> Georgina Blackwell wanted to be a lawyer, but when her mother, a beautician, broke her wrist, Georgina put her dreams on hold and stepped in to help keep her mother's beauty salon going. Five years later her mother's home and business were put at risk in an access dispute with a multinational housing company which wanted to build new luxury homes next door. The developer believed it had right of access across the Blackwells' garden and put scaffolding in their garden in order to demolish the factory next door. The Blackwells found their garden boarded over, their plants destroyed, their business disrupted and their house filled with dust. Georgina's mother took the developer to court, and lost. Ordered to pay damages and legal costs, she faced bankruptcy. It was at that point that Georgina decided she was not going to see her mother suffer any longer, if she could possibly help it. So she plucked up her courage, borrowed law books from the library and fought the case herself. In court she opened the case, gave evidence and cross-examined the developer's solicitor. At the end of the case the judge ruled in the Blackwells' favour and ordered the developer to pay compensation.

Georgina Blackwell proved her love for her mother not once but twice, first by stepping in when her mother broke her wrist, and then by standing up to the developer and going to court to fight her case. After her brave stand she declared that she might now, after all, go to university to study law. With her compassion, courage and sharp intelligence, she would make a great lawyer.

So often we find we can do extraordinary things for those we love. As parents we would move heaven and earth for our children. I have come across many instances of parents of disabled children who have shown extraordinary courage, tenacity, endurance and sacrifice, all in the name of love. Love brings out the very best in us, and as parents we are repaid with great joy as we watch our children grow. But love also requires that we let go of those we love, and this is especially true for parents.

My wife Elizabeth and I are very fortunate to have five healthy and independently-minded children. For us the life and love of our family has been the true north of our compass. We often speak of our children as 'gifts from God', to be held and nurtured until they are ready, in their own strength and with their own wings, to fly the nest.

If you are blessed with children, then, while each and every day is to be savoured and cherished, your main task is to train them to leave home and go out into the world as confident and responsible adults. My wife is wise when she reminds me that if we hold onto them too tightly and fail to teach them to fly, then they will never have the wings to return.

There are many kinds of letting go required of us when we love. Sending our children out into the world when they are ready is one. Releasing a lover, partner or friend when a relationship is not thriving or healthy is another. Allowing someone who is unnecessarily dependent to stand on their own two feet is another. And forgiving those who have hurt us is also a form of letting go, for when we forgive we let go of bitterness, resentment and hatred.

We all, at various times throughout the course of our lives, make mistakes. Sometimes they are huge mistakes. Indeed, who has not said to themselves, 'Why on earth did I do that? How could I possibly have been so stupid?' Deep remorse grips us and we ask ourselves how anyone could trust or respect us again.

But a different attitude can kick in if we can approach those we have hurt or let down and ask for forgiveness and resolution. Jesus said that if you and another person have anything between you which needs to be resolved, then go towards them and ask for their understanding and their forgiveness. And when we finally summon the courage to do that, whatever the response we get, we have the inner knowledge that we have crossed the road and made the effort to be reconciled and forgiven. There is a sense of peace that comes with facing up to our mistakes and doing our best to put right what we have done. And if the other person similarly crosses the road to meet us halfway, then what a sense of relief, of cleansing, of feeling forgiven and renewed will flow through our very being.

If it is hard to admit mistakes and ask for forgiveness, it can be even harder to forgive. If we are the ones being asked to forgive, then we are being offered an opportunity to show love, by letting go of our hurt and anger and choosing reconciliation. When we forgive those who have made mistakes, we acknowledge that we too are human and make mistakes, and we create a bond of humanity with them.

There can perhaps be no harder act to forgive than the murder of your child. Gordon Wilson, a family man who ran a drapery business in his home town of Enniskillen, Northern Ireland, nonetheless forgave the killers of his daughter Marie. He did so with such grace and generosity that people around the world were touched by it and the Queen even mentioned him in her Christmas Day address.

On Remembrance Day in 1987, Gordon and his youngest daughter Marie, a nurse, stood at the cenotaph in Enniskillen with their friends and neighbours from the town. In the middle of the service of remembrance, a bomb exploded. Gordon and Marie were buried under the rubble of the nearby buildings that had collapsed. Gordon described what happened next, in an interview he gave to the BBC later that same day. 'She held my hand tightly, and gripped me as hard as she could. She said, "Daddy, I love you very much." Those were her exact words to me, and those were the last words I ever heard her say.' To the astonishment of listeners, he went on to add, 'But I bear no ill will. I bear no grudge. Dirty sort of talk is not going to bring her back to life. She was a great wee lassie. She loved her profession. She was a pet. She's dead. She's in heaven and we shall meet again. I will pray for these men tonight and every night.' As historian Jonathan Bardon later said, 'No words in more than twenty-five years of violence in Northern Ireland had such a powerful, emotional impact.'

Marie Wilson was one of eleven people who died that day. Her loss shattered Gordon and his wife Joan, but they were anxious that bitterness and hatred should not rip the town apart. Before the bomb, Protestants and Catholics in Enniskillen had lived side by side, and the Wilsons wanted it to stay that way. Gordon Wilson later pleaded with loyalists not to take revenge on the Irish Republican Army members who had been behind the bombing. Throughout the rest of his life, he worked hard to bring about reconciliation between opposing sides in Northern Ireland. He met several times with Loyalist paramilitaries in an attempt to persuade them to abandon violence and he eventually came face to face with the people who had planned the Enniskillen bombing. They apologised for killing Marie. Gordon Wilson died in 1995, but even after his death many people carried on his work. Today in Northern Ireland, the bombings and shootings have stopped, in large part thanks to the work of people like Gordon Wilson.

To show love towards your enemies is an act of great humanity and compassion. Those, like Gordon Wilson, who can forgive where forgiveness seems impossible set a standard we can only attempt to follow.

In his address to the National Prayer Breakfast in Washington DC shortly after his inauguration, President Barack Obama described the need to care for, live alongside and, when necessary, to be reconciled with our fellow human beings in this way:

Jesus told us to 'love thy neighbour as thyself', the Jewish Torah commands, 'that which is hateful to you, do not do to your fellow', in Islam there is the Hadith that reads 'none of you truly believes until he wishes for his brother what he wishes for himself' and the same is true for Buddhists and Hindus; for followers of Confucius and Humanists. It is, of course, the golden rule, the call to love one another; to understand one another; to treat with dignity and respect those with whom we share a brief moment on this earth.

It is an ancient rule; a simple rule; but also one of the most challenging. For it asks each of us to take some measure of responsibility for the well being of people we may not know or worship with or agree with on every issue. Sometimes, it asks us to reconcile with bitter enemies or resolve ancient hatreds. And that requires a living, breathing, active faith. It requires us not only to believe, but to do – to give something of ourselves for the benefit of others and the betterment of our world.

God is love

Frère Roger of Taizé told us, '"God is Love." If we can grasp only those three words we shall go far, very far.' In other words, each of us at whatever age and stage of our life has the opportunity to re-examine our lives and so perhaps for the first time to reach our own conclusions and decisions and to realise that it is never too soon or too late to become the person whom God created us to be.

Jesus went to incredible lengths in order to persuade his hearers and followers of how much God loved them. Over and over again he encouraged men and women to recognise the urgency and importance of feeling known and loved by God.

Amongst those sayings which the Gospel writers recorded are these:

> The kingdom of heaven is like treasure hidden in a field. When a man found it, he hid it again, and then in his joy went and sold all he had and bought that field.
>
> Again, the kingdom of heaven is like a merchant looking for fine pearls. When he found one of great value, he went away and sold everything he had and bought it. (Matt. 13:44–46)

When you realise, perhaps for the first time, that you are known and loved by God and that he does indeed have a purpose for your life, that is the moment when unconditional love connects with the human heart.

To return to President Obama, at the National Prayer Breakfast he described his experience of this love connection:

> I believe that good is possible because my faith teaches me that all is possible. I also believe because of what I have seen and what I have lived. I was not raised in a particularly

religious household. I had a father who was born a Muslim but became an atheist, grandparents who were non-practising Methodists and Baptists and a mother who was sceptical of organised religion, even though she was the kindest, most spiritual person I've ever known. She was the one who taught me as a child to love, and to understand, and to do unto others as I would want done.

I didn't become a Christian until many years later, when I moved to the south side of Chicago after college. It happened not because of indoctrination or a sudden revelation, but because I spent month after month working with church folks who simply wanted to help neighbours who were down on their luck – no matter what they looked like, or where they came from, or who they prayed to. It was on those streets, in those neighbourhoods, that I first heard God's Spirit beckon me. It was there that I felt called to a higher purpose – his purpose.

When I was training for the ministry of the Church of Scotland, one of my mentors was the legendary Second World War padre and chaplain to the Queen in Scotland, Dr Ronnie Selby Wright. He would gather us to discuss how things were going in the parish and he told us many times of St Clement, an early Christian martyr in Rome, who on the night before he died was ordered to assemble all the riches of the church. The next morning on the temple steps he assembled the sick and the sad, the blind and the lame, the poor and the helpless. 'These', said St Clement to his persecutors, 'are the treasures of the church.' And so are we, for in his infinite love, God reminds us, through the life of Jesus of Nazareth, of his great Love.

The recognition that you are no longer a two-dimensional person of mind and body alone, but also have a deep inner spiritual need and capability, is enormously exciting. It is then, according to the life and example of Jesus of Nazareth, that you can indeed be truly loving and loved and lovable.

One of the most beautiful passages about love ever written comes from St Paul's letter to the Corinthians.

> If I speak in the tongues of men and of angels, but have not love, I am only a resounding gong or a clanging cymbal. If I have the gift of prophecy and can fathom all mysteries and all knowledge, and if I have a faith that can move mountains, but have not love, I am nothing. If I give all I possess to the poor and surrender my body to the flames, but have not love, I gain nothing.
>
> Love is patient, love is kind. It does not envy, it does not boast, it is not proud. It is not rude, it is not self-seeking, it is not easily angered, it keeps no record of wrongs. Love does not delight in evil but rejoices with the truth. It always protects, always trusts, always hopes, always perseveres.
>
> Love never fails . . . And now these three remain: faith, hope and love. But the greatest of these is love. (1 Cor. 13:1–13)

Henry Drummond, reflecting on this great hymn of love, wrote:

> The test of a man is not 'how have I believed' but 'how have I loved?' The test of religion, the final test of religion, is not religiousness, but love . . . not what I have done, not what I have believed, not what I have achieved, but how I have discharged the common charities of life. Be not deceived. The words which all of us shall one day hear, sound not of theology but of life, not of churches and saints but of the hungry and the poor, not of creeds and doctrines but of shelter and clothing, not of Bibles and Prayer Books but of cups of cold water in the name of Christ.
>
> Who is Christ? He who fed the hungry, clothed the naked,

visited the sick. And where is Christ? Where? – whoever receives a little child in my name receives me. And who are Christ's? Everyone that loves is born of God.[6]

In the end, the quality and power of love, God's love, is the greatest spiritual resource of all.

Reflections

To feel fully alive we need to know not merely that we are loving, but also that we are loved because we are truly lovable. Spend time discarding those negatives from your background and past which may be holding you back. Embrace a whole new way of looking at things, like a newly-born child crying out, 'I want to love and be loved.'

Give generously of your love to others, through caring for them, listening, helping and supporting. And never be afraid to let go, when letting go is the right thing to do.

Thank God that he knows you, every part of you, within and without – that he still loves you and wants the very best for you and for your life. Then ask him to help you grasp the immensity of his faith and his hope and his love in you.

Strength with the weak
Gentleness with the violent
Give to us O God the leadership of Columba
Love for the unlovely
Hope for the hopeless
Give to us O God the leadership of Christ
What we never dared
What we never tried
What we never believed
Give to us O God the leadership
That might be ours

May this place touch all who come here with the spirit of
    Christ who has shown the way to true leadership
in the way of humble service. Amen

(This Columban Prayer of Dedication, by The Right Rev.
Andrew McLellan, Moderator of the General Assembly of the
Church of Scotland, was first given in the presence of HRH
The Princess Royal on the occasion of the official opening of
Columba 1400 on 3 June 2000.)

Endnotes

Serenity

1. Overwork Blamed for Medical Errors, Daily Telegraph, April 13th 2009.
http://www.telegraph.co.uk/health/healthnews/5147744/Overwork-blamed.

2. Gaby Hinscliff Quits Work, Observer, November 1st 2009
http://www.guardian.co.uk/culture/2009/nov/01/gaby-hinsliff-quits-work. Used with permission

3. ibid

Purpose

1. Quote from the Dalai Lama, source unknown.

2. Chariots of Fire, 20th Century Fox Home Entertainment/ Enigma Productions 1981

Service

1. Frère Roger, Letter from Taize, Copyright ©Ateliers et Presses de Taizé, 71250 Taizé, France.

2. John Carlin, The Independent, 1994. Used with permission

3. Bishop Ken Untener of Saginaw, 1979

Wisdom before Knowledge

1. Ron Ferguson, The Herald. March 5th 2007. Used with permission

2. Anthem, Leonard Cohen, Sony/ATV Music Publishing (UK) Limited, 2009.

3. Hope, R. S. Thomas, Orion Publishing Group, 1981, Used by permission.
4. Tension, Joy Cowley Psalms Down Under, Pleroma Press, Otane 1996
5. NPR Interview in 1994 – National Public Radio
6. I have a dream . . . Andersson / Ulvaeus, Bocu Music. Used by permission.

Faith

1. Lance Armstrong , It's Not About the Bike: My Journey Back to Life, G.P Putnam's Sons 2000.
2. The Scottish Himalayan Experience, W. H. Murray, J.M. Dent & Sons (London) 1951,
3. Wisdom from World Religions: Pathways towards Heaven on Earth, John Templeton, Templeton Foundation Press, 2002

Hope

1. Vaclav Havel, www.vaclavehavel.cz.
2. Frère Roger, Letter from Taize, Copyright ©Ateliers et Presses de Taizé, 71250 Taizé, France.
3. Footprints, author unknown

Love

1. Frère Roger, Letter from Taize, Copyright ©Ateliers et Presses de Taizé, 71250 Taizé, France.
2. ibid.
3. Quote attributed to Father Alfred D'Souza d.2004.
4. The Greatest Thing in the World, Henry Drummond, Hodder & Stoughton, 2009. Used by permission

If you have enjoyed reading *The Power of 3* and found it beneficial then you may wish to consider attending an accompanying retreat.

Retreats, either one to one with Norman Drummond or within a small group setting, offer the time and space to explore each of the themes in more depth.

If you would like further information regarding these retreats or Norman Drummond's work, please visit the Drummond International web-site www.drummondinternational.com or e-mail info@drummondinternational.com.

If you are interested in finding out more about Columba 1400 then please visit www.columba1400.com.